With God's Help Flowers Bloom

With God's Help Flowers Bloom

Elaine Anderson

QUALITY PUBLICATIONS
P.O. BOX 1060 ABILENE, TEXAS 79604

ACKNOWLEDGEMENTS

Permissions:

Pass It On by Kurt Kaiser, Copyright © 1969 by Lexicon Music, Inc. All rights reserved. International copyright secured. Used by special permission. Performance rights licensed through ASCAP.

"Cause and Effect" from *Dare To Be Happy* by Helen Lowrie Marshall. Copyright © 1962 by Helen Lowrie Marshall. Required by permission of Doubleday & Company, Inc.

"Point of View" and "The Greatest of These" from *Aim For A Star* by Helen Lowrie Marshall. Copyright © 1964 by Helen Lowrie Marshall. Reprinted by permission of Doubleday & Company, Inc.

From *The New International Version, New Testament*. Copyright © 1973 by The New York Bible Society International. Used by permission.

From *The Amplified Bible, Old Testament,* Copyright © 1962, 1964 by Zondervan Publishing House. Used by permission.

From *The Living Bible, Paraphrased*, Copyright © 1971 by Tyndale House Publishers. Used by permission.

ISBN: 0-89137-411-6

Acknowledgements

In the fabric of a person's life, God has seen fit to weave some special golden threads. These give the material its beauty and strength. They are the part that makes the material useable. Looking back I can see so clearly the ones who, sometimes unknowingly and other times purposely, have been those threads in my life. God, the Master Weaver, created a design and these special people were willing to be used for His purpose. How great the heavenly Artist is!

It is with deep gratitude that I want to acknowledge these wonderful people and the help they gave me:

My mother and father who, above all else that they gave, taught me to count on God by the way they lived their life.

My husband, Bill, who gave me his unconditional love which constantly encourages and strengthens me.

Wanda Leppanen, the friend who is always there with love, support, and the constant reminder that God IS able.

Kathy and Karen, our daughters, such precious girls - who cleaned house, washed clothes, and tip-toed through the house while the "writer" wrote.

Judy Phillips, who managed to turn my scribbled notes into a perfectly typed manuscript.

Paul Magee, who taught us beautiful lessons about God's love and grace.

Mickey Gilliland and his wife Betty, who believed in me and convinced me I had something worthwhile to share.

Joann Chappell, Mary McIlroy, and my sister - Libby Palmer, who kept me going with their love and prayers as I wrote and rewrote.

John and Johnny Barhydt, and Gene Basford, who made it possible for me to see this book in print for the first time when we printed copies for a ladies' retreat.

The Elders and members of the Florissant Church of Christ, for their acceptance and love.

Marge Green and Ona Belknap, who told me to keep trying when I became discouraged about getting the book published.

Lil Rodgers, Pat White, and all the other ladies in our classes who kept telling me the material was worthwhile.

God bless you all and may you continue to be golden threads in the fabric of God's plan for other Christians.

Elaine Anderson

Introduction

In 1970 while I was the secretary for the Florissant Church of Christ, a book came in the mail for our minister, Mickey Gilliland. Many books passed across my desk there at the church building, but this one particularly caught my attention. It was written for Christian women who are married to non-Christians.

Since I had married a non-Christian and was fully aware of the tremendous struggles in this kind of marriage, I took the book home to read. I remember wondering as I read, if this book would have helped me during the 10 years that Bill wasn't a Christian. There were a lot of problems that I faced during those years - problems within myself, problems that I had struggled to find answers for. But this book was not written for the purpose of speaking to those problems. I was disappointed as I knew many ladies that could use that kind of help right now. I talked to Mickey about it. He asked me what I would say if I wrote a book to ladies married to non-Christians. We talked about it quite a lot, and he encouraged me to write my thoughts into book form.

What an idea! I couldn't really imagine myself writing anything - much less a book. But the idea kept persisting as I talked to Bill and others about the idea. At this time Bill had been a Christian for seven years. We discussed the years before he became a Christian and he encouraged me to go ahead and write the book.

So I began writing and gathering material. Through the years many books and classes had helped me - so I read those books again, talked to the teachers, and went through the notes I had kept. After a lot of crying, praying, and hard work

I finally finished. But the book hadn't been tested yet and I wondered how the material would be accepted. So I sent out questionnaires to the ladies from our area churches. And they graciously responded. They agreed with my thoughts and by their answers encouraged me to continue. I shall always be grateful for their honesty and candor.

At this time I was asked to teach a ladies' class at church using the material from the book. I was not only excited - I was scared to death. But with a lot of help I began and these classes continued for four years. During the classes a certain method of arrangement and teaching evolved. These classes were called "With God's Help" classes and you can read more specifically about their make-up in the study guide for classes which is being published separately. During this time God saw fit to push me along a little further by way of a neighbor who insisted WE begin a Bible study. I eventually became the leader in this study and when we finished our first topic, we then went into a study of the book material. I used the same class format as we had used at church. We had some wonderful lessons both at church and in the neighborhood - and I was soon forced to see that the material prepared for women married to non-Christians was also very necessary for all women. We all need to find a more fulfilled life through finding God's help. Women today desperately need to build a relationship to God and to find out that what He says will make us happy.

I pray that you will find a new joy in your life through the study and use of the chapters of this book. Please study it carefully, always looking for truth, and always rejecting untruth. We have studied and prayed over the material here, that it be strong and true, containing no error. The elders of the Florissant church have read it for accuracy, as have others.

The Scriptures have been printed in different versions, depending upon which read the clearest. No version is perfect; all contain errors in translation, so you should always exercise care in your study and should do as I have - choose the reading that will best reach out to your heart with the truth that God is giving us. Let it speak to you, no matter where you are in your walk with God, so you will become familiar with exactly what God is saying to you.

The stories, thoughts and ideas that I have written about are a sharing of what I have seen as my biggest struggles. I take no credit for this sharing; I only praise Him for pushing me forward, always providing the abundant help I needed. I was for many years very stubborn, very independent and very weak in faith. I had such a struggle because there were always two forces deep within me - AND THEY ARE ALSO WITHIN YOU: a basic need to have God active in my life and yet a burning desire to do things my own way. I always wanted to figure out what was best for my life - MYSELF. Each conflict remains imprinted upon my mind in great detail. I have tried to capture their basic content for you but I know that I have not been able to relay adequately the very real personal struggles - some very painful to remember. I tried so hard to resist God. I almost passed up the real happiness that comes from giving in to God on each and every issue individually.

There are times when I still am weak and faithless and stubborn. And it is because of these human faults that I have had such a struggle. You may also see within yourself the same human faults that will cause you to fight against and strongly resist allowing God to mold you and make you into the happy woman He wants you to be.

So if a chapter seems to sound like I am admonishing, it is first to myself and then to you that I am saying strongly, TRUST GOD. And remember, these are the steps you took - steps that need to be repeated and repeated each day with each problem for the rest of your life and mine.

Begin searching your life to see where you are in relationship to God. Take one day at a time and rebuild it into God's way. And when you forget and slip back - start over again with the next problem, trying again to follow God's way instead of your own. And He will help you, most generously, over-abundantly, because He loves you. That is the whole idea in this book.

I have hoped in writing this book to answer these questions: (1) Where can today's woman really find a fulfilling, exciting and challenging happiness? (2) How can marriage today, in our fast-paced, modern society, be not only successful - but wonderfully happy? (3) How can a Christian pass on to someone else the wonderful news of Christianity?

The answer I give to these questions is, WITH GOD'S HELP . . . With God's help the woman can bloom; the flower in all its beauty can be called to the purpose for which it was made. God's help is specific, strong, and reliable. And there are very definite ways for the woman to find His help:

First, it is essential that you establish a relationship with God and learn His will for you. You can do this by studying what He has said about the specific areas of your life. Then you can learn how to have an open line of communication with Him. This will enable you to look to Him for the special and specific problems in your life.

Second, you should be able to turn to your Christian friends for the strengthening of your faith as you learn how they have received and understood God's help - how they have stumbled, and how much they really do love you and each other.

All of this brings the woman to a point of understanding that she may have seen dimly in the distance before; but now she can see clearly that God loves her, that he is wondrously able to help, that He is very much in control, and, finally, that above all He is an infinitely precious gift to share with someone else. As you are able to apply each chapter to your life, to look at yourself to see if you are mirroring what God wants, improving with time, finding the marvelous happiness that comes from living God's way...
...then you can begin to pass it on to someone else.

God is so great, He must be shared! Then we will see many more flowers BLOOM.

Table of Contents

With God's Help

Chapter 1

A young mother believing she had an incurable disease walked onto the Eads bridge and jumped into the muddy, cold waters of the Mississippi River. Some men saw her jump and quickly set out after her in a small rowboat moored nearby. Looking toward the area where she hit the water, they saw her head and heard her scream for help, but didn't reach her in time. The murky water pulled her under as they helplessly watched from a distance. Slowly and sadly, the men made their way back to the river bank.

Two weeks later a church in the area donated a small motor boat which could be used for faster rescues in case anyone else attempted suicide from that bridge. Everyone was filled with despair that there was no help available that was fast enough or strong enough to reach the twenty-three year old mother of three. How sad that although she didn't want to die, she didn't know what else to do.

The threat of incurable illness provokes a feeling of fear, desperation, and helplessness. This young mother gave up, rather than fight what she saw as a hopeless battle against cancer. And surely part of her decision to give up was the belief that, although there was a possibility of winning, the fight would require too much from her. But then after making her decision to jump and after feeling the icy waters encircle her, she apparently changed her mind because she began screaming for help. At that point if there had been help available that was suited to the task, she could have been saved.

We are much the same. Hopelessness can enter the life of the Christian. We often find that life is full of problems that

1

we cannot handle, or we feel that we would have to give up too much in order to solve a problem. Perhaps we just don't have enough information available about how to tackle a bad situation. We need help but because it isn't "readily available", we are many times lost because we don't see the answers as workable solutions that will make us better off than we were. When we get right to the point—we face hopelessness because being a Christian isn't helping us as it should.

There are many examples of Christians who have to face this hopelessness without help. One such story is about a lady named Marge. One Sunday Marge walked into church as usual, but instead of sitting near one of her friends, she sat down by herself. This was a little out of the ordinary but not enough that anyone would really notice. Marge felt numb. She didn't want to visit with anyone or have anyone notice how she felt. Marge had just learned that her daughter, a senior in high school, was pregnant and didn't even know who the father was. Marge sat there in the church auditorium and wondered where she had failed. The singing began so she sang also. She bowed her head when prayer was led. She sat and listened to the sermon, sang again when the service was ending, then got up and quietly slipped out. As she was driving home she thought about how her own marriage had ended in divorce; now her daughter was pregnant and unmarried; her life seemed full of failure. Yet Marge had been a Christian since she was a teenager. She had faithfully attended all of the services of the church, even teaching Bible class for many years. She had lived as good a life as she knew how and yet as she looked back, it all seemed to be worth absolutely nothing. Marge decided that she wouldn't go back to church.

Another Christian, a young man I had known for years, faced hopelessness also—only in a different way. His wife wasn't a Christian. One Sunday he came to visit the congregation where we now attend, and, after services, came over to talk to us. He spoke in desperation. His wife refused to let him bring the children to church. "What should I do?" he asked. We introduced him to people and encouraged him to come back, hoping perhaps that a change in churches might bring his wife to worship. A few weeks later I saw him again. "Please pray for me," he said. "I'm having a meeting tonight with my wife and her family and we are going to talk about church. Perhaps we can agree on something." We all prayed for Dan but his situation was not to be remedied at this late date. His wife absolutely refused to let him bring the children to church and he couldn't stand that. He issued an ultimatum to that effect, so she left him. They are now divorced and she has the children all of the time. Nothing was gained and everything was lost because of hopelessness.

My own story also points out a need for help. I had been a Christian from a very young age and I had attended the services of the church quite regularly until a time in 1960. After three years of marriage (which seemed headed for divorce) and with a husband who was totally uninterested in changing, I felt quite hopeless. I knew that my Christianity wasn't helping me so I left the church. I knew that I should be attending services, but I just could not continue going to a church that wasn't helping me. In fact I usually left church feeling a lot worse. Everyone in the church that I had been attending seemed to know exactly what to do to please God. And if they saw anyone else doing what they regarded as unpleasing to God—they let them know about it in no uncertain terms. I knew I needed help, but somehow I also knew that if I asked, the answers would be, "Keep coming to church, trust in God, live a good Christian life, and don't give up." Now of course there is nothing wrong with that advice, but at the time I needed much more than that. I didn't know HOW to have faith, or HOW to live a "Christian" life, or WHY I should keep coming to a church that only added to my misery because of its self-righteousness. I needed more power than was available there.

What is the answer for Christians in these positions? We know that the help needs to be strong and powerful, suited to the task before it. Some people believe that prayer is the only answer. So when they have problems they pray and hope, cry and wait. They don't give up, but nothing seems to happen to change their lives. We know that "all things work together for good to those who love the Lord" and "the Holy Spirit helps us with our daily problems and in our praying." Why then with all of this does it take so long for results to be seen? When I asked other women this question they said that "God moves in mysterious ways and has his own time for everything. We should pray and wait, remain patient and let time take care of everything." But is this really the answer? It wasn't in my life.

And I would certainly agree with all who say that "giving up" is certainly not the answer. Marge's life didn't get any better after she left the church. And the young man who wanted his children raised in the church certainly gained nothing by force or giving up.

I didn't give up. I had tried seven years of praying and waiting. That didn't work. So being persistent by nature I guess it was only natural that I didn't quit. Although I quit coming to church, thanks to my parents and the training they had given me about trusting in God, I continued to hope that God would help me. Yet our life seemed to be the same. One evening after watching television together and then arguing about religion, Bill proclaimed that he would never be a Christian. Crushed, I got up from the easy chair and went into our dark bedroom, knelt beside the bed, and began praying in a different way.

A few days earlier a verse had been brought to my attention by a friend.

> If you want to know what God wants you to do, ask him, and he will gladly tell you, for he is always ready to give a bountiful supply of wisdom to all who ask him; he will not resent it (James 1:5 LB).

So I prayed, "God, I'm not doing the right thing. Please let me know what I'm doing wrong." And into my head popped the picture of Jesus with his arms outstretched to the little children. "He cares," I thought. And I arose full of the assurance that God would somehow let me know what I had been doing wrong.

AND HE DID! My "bountiful supply" of wisdom that I had asked for came to me in a variety of ways—MOST OF THEM PAINFUL. I learned that, although I thought I was a Christian because I had been baptized into the body, no one could see Christ in me. I also saw that, although I had judged the church for being self-righteous, I had been just as self-righteous in my actions toward my husband. You see, I thought I was doing a good job as a Christian simply because I "didn't do" many things that Christians aren't supposed to do. And I had looked upon my husband's "un-Christianity" with condemnation. Oh, how it hurt to realize that actually my husband had a much more "Christlike" personality than I. He was never unkind to me, or inconsiderate, or "preachy." Another sore spot was the fact that I had not been obeying God's will in my life, especially when it came to being an "adapting, submissive wife." My life showed no faith in God's love either, because I demonstrated no happiness in being a Christian. And I began to understand that when someone sees an unhappy Christian they are not too inclined to look further into becoming one themselves. The wisdom I was given was only the beginning.

Now I saw that I needed to change, but I knew that I needed help with that also. God answered that need too. God's help has made it possible for me and for many others like me to climb the steps of life in a different way, dealing with the problems along the way while showing others just how great it is to be a Christian. Because of God's help in changing me and in working in my husband's life, he became a Christian two years later. So we both found God's help.

But I believe that Bill and I were lucky. Not all Christians are as persistant as we are. Not all Christians have had the training in faith that I had received from my parents. Marge, Dan, and I have all had the same problem though. We didn't know how to apply our faith to life's problems in a specific way. As with all Christians, we accepted God and our need for Him when we became Christians. We knew we couldn't get into heaven by ourselves. We placed the cross of Christ, our only hope, on the horizon of our mind. And there it stayed until problems arose and life began to surround us. Then the cross slowly faded from our view. We forgot God's promises to help us. We instead tried to handle situations according to our own power and thought. Then, after we had eventually failed, we turned to Him. And each one of us will eventually fail simply because no one is capable of handling all that life may hand out—without God's help.

And then when we reach our point of need, we often don't know how to find the help that God offers. One reason many Christians end up relying on themselves is because they don't

know how to SPECIFICALLY apply the principles of faith
which we once accepted into our everyday life. It's hard to
know how to "love our neighbor" when their children are
beating up on our children. It's terribly difficult to know how
to handle a situation when someone in our family is
demanding, critical, or unconcerned about how we feel. Then
all we want to do is react. And the reaction is usually not the
way God would want us to react. What would God have us do?
This question needs to be answered continually in all aspects
of our life. We need to hear from other members of our
Christian family about how they handled their problems and
about how they put their faith into practice. We need more
information.

We need information just as the young mother who jumped
to her death. She probably had some facts about how the
disease of cancer is treated. She had probably heard about
people who had the cancer "cut" out, people who were
disfigured for life. She had probably also heard from
someone, "Have faith in your doctor." But that wasn't
enough help for her. She could have gained more knowledge
from different sources; but she wasn't persistant by nature.
She gave up. Yet when her body was found, two months
later, an autopsy showed that SHE DIDN'T HAVE CANCER
AT ALL.

And the problems that Christians experience aren't a cancer
either. Yet because as Christians we often wear a mask that
covers up our troubles, our sorrows, our searchings, our
growth, and our strengths, we do not really have complete
knowledge either. We come to church wearing our very best
clothes, our very best faces, and our very best dispositions.
We do not reveal ourselves to one another and therefore we
aren't revealing the extent of our need. Some Christians are
crying out for more information, for help with their faith, for a
look into another Christian's life. Because we don't know each
other, we can't pray specifically for each other. And because
we don't understand each other's problems, we can't love each
other as much as when we do know. Many people come to
church and leave feeling that apparently they aren't handling
life as well as the "good" Christians here. They feel there
must be something drastically wrong with them. And there
isn't.

If we only knew—we would help. We would share. We would tell you that we have had the same searching, the same questions, the same needs. I hope this book will in some small way convey this to you. I hope we can keep hopelessness from building into a disease that can't be helped. This is what happened in my own life. Actually no one thing was really hopeless. It was putting them all together, then having no answers for them, and feeling the frustration of having no specific help, that allowed the little sores to fester until they spread into the whole body. And of course we all know that marriages don't suddenly fall apart; they crumble brick by brick. Raising good strong children happens not because of luck, but because of a series of proper decisions. Similarly the help we need can be applied in a step by step way. Then it is really strong and able to pull us from our hopelessness.

God's help is adequate and strong enough for any task as long as we understand that it is available for us. The church can provide this information by offering classes such as the ones we have had for several years; classes that give individuals the opportunity to express the needs they have and which also allow each of us to tell about God's help in our lives. Individual Christians can also provide the same kind of help for each other, by either providing "With God's Help" classes in their homes, or by simply explaining about God's help to people who ask. But most of all we can each demonstrate our faith in God's help in our daily lives. In whichever case, we would then be offering the best possible help; help that will remove the fear of fighting the battle, remove the dread of years spend having "different" feelings than anyone else (when in reality we all have the same problems), remove from within the reach of individuals who feel hopeless the "icy waters of giving up," remove the CANCER that is eating away at the hearts of many Christians - the fact that they don't know how to have God's help with life and with life's problems.

HELP

God's Help is Powerful
I pray that you will begin to understand how incredibly great his power is to help those who believe him. It is that same mighty power that raised Christ from the dead and seated him in the place of honor at God's right hand in heaven, far, far above any other king or ruler or dictator or leader . . . (Ephesians 1:19-21a LB.)

Mighty Power
And God has reserved for his children the priceless gift of eternal life; it is kept in heaven for you, pure and undefiled, beyond the reach of change and decay. And God, in his mighty power, will make sure that you get there safely to receive it, because you are trusting him. It will be yours in that coming last day for all to see. So be truly glad! There is wonderful joy ahead, even though the going is rough for a while down here (1 Peter 1:4-6 LB).

Through The Bible
Nothing is perfect except your words. Oh, how I love them. I think about them all day long. They make me wiser than my enemies, because they are my constant guide. Yes, wiser than my teachers, for I am ever thinking of your rules (Psalms 119:96-99 LB).
(Read also Psalms 119:100-106)

Gain Wisdom and Understanding
If you want to know what God wants you to do, ask him, and he will gladly tell you, for he is always ready to give a bountiful supply of wisdom to all who ask him; he will not resent it (James 1:5 LB).

Pray and Sing Praises to the Lord
Is anyone among you suffering? He should keep on praying about it. And those who have reason to be thankful should continually be singing praises to the Lord (James 5:13 LB).

Help Each Other
Now we ask you, brothers, to respect those who work hard among you, who are over you in the Lord and who

admonish you. Hold them in the highest regard in love because of their work. Live in peace with each other. And we urge you, brothers, warn those who are idle, encourage the timid, help the weak, be patient with everyone. Make sure that nobody pays back wrong for wrong, but always try to be kind to each other and to everyone else (1 Thessalonians 5:12-15 NIV).

Love Each Other

Little children, let us stop just saying we love people; let us **really** love them, and **show it** by our **actions** (1 John 3:18 LB).

Happiness

Chapter 2

Let's think for a moment about the Christian who has not reached a point of hopelessness but who doesn't have that wonderful happiness that comes from having God's help in their life. We all want to be happy. We begin looking for happiness almost as soon as we are born. And our search for happiness reminds me of a story I heard once.

A young man walked up to his father and said, "I must leave our house and go in search of happiness." With great excitement he told his father, "There are great lands, towering mountains, deep colored oceans and sparkling streams that beckon to me. There are fascinating people to meet, different things to see, and places I must visit. I know that out there I shall find the happiness I am seeking." Later the boy returned. His father looked at him and said, "Son, I see by the smile on your face that in your travels you found happiness. Tell me, what country held the joy you were looking for? What people gave you the answer to your searching?" The boy, still smiling, said, "Father, I did find happiness, but not in any of the places where I looked. I found that happiness was with me all the time. It was inside of me."

This is a simple story, but very true. We all want very much to have inner happiness and we search for it in many places throughout our lives. We look for pleasurable experiences, for new and exciting challenges, for freedom, for peace of mind, and for anything else which seems likely to furnish what we need. From the time as tiny babies when we answer the need for food and comfort as we snuggle at mother's breast, to the times when we are growing up and reaching for the bright and shiny toys, or choosing our friends to play with, we are exploring and moving toward whatever gives us pleasure. I am always reminded of this continuing search when I see the senior high students driving past our house as they leave for school each day. The back of our home sits on one of the main roads from the largest high school in St. Louis. And I see them piled together into souped-up cars, sometimes with arms and legs dangling out of windows. They are happy just being free. They are excited to be with their friends and find a lot of happiness is just doing what everyone else is doing. I can still (unfortunately) remember some of the daring, exciting, and perhaps stupid things we did when we were that age. But at the same time pleasure seemed to be the answer to happiness; then, thankfully, as maturity and growth added to our knowledge, most of us chose a role in life that offered more than just pleasure. We wanted something dependable. And most people eventually make these more obvious choices in the search for a lasting happiness: marriage, raising children, an education, a job, and other responsible choices.

But another factor besides wanting dependability enters into our hunt for happiness. Our individual background and training plays an important role in what choices we make. A young farm girl who grows up in the country and is influenced strongly by a father who believes a woman should not work outside of the home will find it hard to obtain happiness by breaking away from her own upbringing and from the guidelines which were set by her parents. Of course, some people only find happiness by rebelling - but that is another story. On the most part we each settle for choices that are agreeable with how we were raised. For example, I was brought up by Christian parents who placed great emphasis on the importance of Christianity. My husband's parents believed in the importance of the family and their daily life stressed that belief. So Bill and I have brought both of these things into our marriage. And I am convinced that neither of us could find real happiness outside of the horizon that was formed for us by our parents in the training years. Only a great deal of force can change this horizon for anyone.

Add to this limitation in finding real happiness another important and immovable frame—our individual need to be who we are. Each of us is unique. We were born that way. So this difference makes our search for happiness quite individualized. My needs are different than your needs. Some people enjoy a busy day, others like the quiet times. Some people are happier taking things apart and putting them back together again. Others enjoy looking at a whole object and studying its relationship to the world around it. Again, to use our own lives as examples, I can recall being painfully shy, introverted, and very fearful of new things. Books were a constant and safe source of pleasure to me. Bill was just the opposite. Friendly, outgoing, a smiling extrovert, he made friends with everyone and was much too busy to read. Again, our individual search for happiness had boundaries that we could not change. We are who we are.

Even though our search for happiness has limitations, with determination many people find what seems to be the happiness they want, until something happens to change it. Surely you have seen the marriage that lost its luster, but the couple did not decide to call it quits; they simply switched their emphasis and effort to another area. (Subconsciously we have all done this kind of switching throughout our lives as our needs changed, as we matured, as we obtained more knowledge, or as we found failure in our original choice for happiness.) But in this marriage that is floundering, the husband begins spending all of his time doing other things which he enjoys, perhaps fishing, or reading or overhauling cars, or having the nights out with the fellows—anything that will keep him happy in an unhappy situation. You've also seen the housewife who devotes all of her time to re-decorating the house, or to keeping busy in "church" work, or in going back to work, or by finding some hobby that occupies her mind—anything that keeps an already unhappy situation from seeming so bad. And I hasten to add that of course none of these things that the man or his wife have chosen as a replacement are wrong - we all enjoy temporary happiness. They fill many of our needs. But the problem is this: They can cover up the real vacancy that is present in our lives. We may switch from one choice to another in our struggle for happiness simply because none of the original choices were lasting, dependable, or strong.

Instead, they are temporary; they are not dependable. They could change with the years. They can lose their appeal. They do not always adjust to our own peculiar needs. And they can cover up the emptiness. A friend once described this as being on a merry-go-round that never stops. We continue to go round and round, changing horses perhaps to relieve the monotony, listening to the music which soothes our ears and keeps them from hearing the inner cry of hunger. And the years pass by and a life becomes used up before we even realize that there is really much more to life.

We just aren't looking in the right place. Everyone has this problem. Each generation has looked for happiness. Each country has tried to control circumstances around it so it could provide more happiness to itself. Moreover each person tries to manage life around him so that the ingredients for a happy life will flow toward him. Yet although each passing century has given us more knowledge and each new set of laws has been passed for the purpose of giving us better lives, better control - all we need to do is look around to see the failure. Wars begin and end. Countries rise and fall. People kill and rob. Watergate told us how our government was inadequate in control. Divorce shows the hopelessness in many marriages. Children are hungry and deprived around the world. Even the Christian family experiences problems and loss of happiness when the pressures and frustrations arise, when the children need more attention than can be given, when the bills can't be paid, when the relatives present problems, when businesses are closed, when food becomes scarce, when marriages crinkle around the edges, when sickness and death interrupt our planning, then we can see that the happinesses we have so pernaciously pursued can fly right out the window. They are not permanent. My own life and the lives of the ladies who have shared in classes give added impact to this knowledge. There is no permanent happiness available in the world.

The only permanent happiness is having the right relationship with God. The boy who went looking for happiness and found it inside of himself had more to say about his search. "Father, the inner happiness I found was given to me by you. Because of the years that you have guided my growth and cared for me I know NOW how much you love me. Because you have taken the time to give me all of the words of wisdom that you know will help me, I can handle life with strength. But also, dear Father, while I was far away, I knew that I could call on you for help and that you would send help. It was then that I realized my inner happiness was with me all the time and that it was a gift from you."

The young boy had the right relationship with his father and because he did, he had been filled with the tremendous knowledge that his father loved him. He had not resisted his father's wisdom and he had not been too proud to realize that he could ask for help if he needed it. Here, also, the Christian needs to find the right relationship with God before he can experience the wonderful inner happiness he wants.

God's love answers the original need in each of us that began when we were born. It adds a new dimension to everything in life. Disappointments are not disappointing anymore because we know that God has our best interest in mind. Problems that come have a different effect on our lives because now we aren't handling them alone anymore. And the small joys and blessings that have always been around are now seen as they were meant to be seen, as gifts from God. What makes the difference? Letting God make the changes in us that we can't make ourselves. Growing and stretching to another step in life by depending upon God's help, instead of depending upon ourselves. Using the wisdom that God has given us in the Bible as a guide for our lives. Drawing close to Him in a very personal relationship through Christ. Accepting the love that He has offered all of His children, the same love that is not understood or accepted by the many unhappy Christians.

God's love changes everything. Pleasure, excitement, challenge, joy, and peace are all constant companions. Our limited horizons are changed by the great power of a loving God. Our "temporary" happiness is deepened into much more as every moment takes on new meaning. Life's problems are answered. We have pleasing relationships with others. We find out who we are. We find great changes in personal growth and development. We see a new ability to respond creatively to the world around us. We have a stability and a constancy that will never leave us even during life's saddest, most sorrowful moments; even when we are frustrated or bored, even when our needs seem immense, even when we have failed. All of this because we have a Father who wants us to have a full, abundant life (John 10:10). He wants you and I to trust him in our times of trouble (Psalms 50:15). He wants us to count on him for each day's living (Colossians 2:6-8). He is a Father who can fill all our needs (Psalms 23:1). And He knows each of us as an individual (Matthew 10:29-31).

So true inner happiness comes from accepting the love and care of God. This love is well described in a story I heard:

A young boy who was very mean was told one day by his mother to do something he didn't want to do. He got pretty mad and after fuming and fretting about how he couldn't possibly do what his mother required, he made a decision. He went into the house and killed his mother. Then not wanting anyone to find out about his evil deed, he cut her into pieces and started carrying her into the woods where he could hide her. But as he was walking over the rough path, he tripped. And the mother's heart fell on the ground at his feet. And as he stooped to pick it up, the heart said, "Did you hurt yourself, son?"

This is the way God loves us. God loves us in spite of who we are (1 John 4:10). He loves us because of who He is (1 John 4:8). (Isn't that a relief?) He has a special love for his children (1 John 3:1), because we love the crucified Son (John 14:21; 16:27). While once we were sinners and outside the family relationship, we are now seen through Christ's death (Isaiah 53:11; 2 Corinthians 5:21; 1 Peter 3:21). We are seen much as we view our children after birth. Before that we didn't really know them. We wanted them but we had to wait until they were born. We are born into God's family (1 Peter 3:21), and as we expect our children to accept our love for them, we should also accept God's love and promise to help us (1 Peter 1:5).

Human nature often causes us to get mean, to fume and fret about something that we know God wants us to do. And many times we make the decision to go against God's will as we see revealed in the Bible. The nature that causes us to do this also caused men to kill God in human form. There were many excuses made about why this happened; the law was being broken, the man has blasphemed God, he had done miracles in God's name, work was done on the Sabbath, and especially, "everybody else was doing it." Yet still God loves us enough to ask us after all of that, "Did you hurt yourself, son?" He loves us enough to promise us eternal salvation if we will only trust His love and power.

So inner happiness becomes real for the Christian who completely and utterly turns his life over to God. Then the

Father who knows us and all of our yearnings can help us become the child he wants us to be. No matter now where we have thought we would find happiness, because God knows better than we do what kind of temporary happiness will really fulfill us. He knows you and I as individuals. He knew that I didn't need to be shy, but that with help could venture to share what He has done for me with others. He knew that I had turned to marriage in my search for happiness and He knew that I would never find real happiness until I stopped trying so hard to figure everything out and just relaxed into doing His will as it applies to marriage. He knew how to help the lady who came to class one evening and, during the course of our conversation, suddenly blurted out her extreme weakness in faith. "I have taught Bible school for years. I have taught your children," she said. "I didn't know my own lack of faith, but lately I have seen that I don't really believe that God is watching over everything." So we prayed together about this with her and a few weeks later she told me what had happened. She came home one night from shopping and just barely caught the telephone ringing. So she rushed in and answered it. The caller told her that although her husband had been transferred out of St. Louis to the Northeast a few weeks ago and they were planning to move soon, one of the men had just quit his job with the company and now her husband would get his job. That doesn't sound so exciting unless you know the background to this story. Both of their parents live in the South and they were being transferred far away from them. Both were unhappy about this. Now they would be transfered to a city only a few miles from both parents. She believed that this was God's answer to her to strengthen her faith. I believe it was too. Many other people have also been strengthened in faith by seeing God's answers to prayer. Many times the answers are not even pleasant but looking back we can see that God is carefully watching over us. He knows our own unique limitations and needs. He knows that the whole world is searching and He has tried to tell everyone that **He** is the only answer. He is not temporary. He is not changeable. He is powerful to help. He helps us because of his great love.

> Love ever gives, forgives, outlives,
> And ever stands with open hands,
> And while it lives, it gives.
> For this is love's perogative
> to GIVE, and GIVE, and GIVE.

HAPPINESS IS:

Knowing God Loves Us

For God loved the world so much that he gave his only Son so that anyone who believes in him shall not perish but have eternal life (John 3:16 LB).

Marvelous Love

And I pray that Christ will be more and more at home in your hearts, living within you as you trust in him. May your roots go down deep into the soil of God's marvelous love, and may you be able to feel and understand, as all God's children should, how long, how wide, how deep, and how high his love really is; and to experience this love for yourselves, though it is so great that you will never see the end of it or fully know or understand it. And so at last you will be filled up with God himself (Ephesians 3:17-19 LB).

God's Love

God showed how much he loved us by sending his only Son into this wicked world to bring to us eternal life through his death. In this act we see what real love is: it is not our love for God, BUT HIS LOVE FOR US when he sent His Son to satisfy God's anger against our sins (1 John 4:9, 10 LB).

Constant Love

For the Lord is always good. He is always loving and kind, and his faithfulness goes on and on to each succeeding generation (Psalms 100:5 LB).

A Father's Love

How great is the love the Father has lavished on us, that we should be called children of God! And that is what we are! (1 John 3:1a NIV).

Happiness Isn't Found in Men

Don't look to men for help; their greatest leaders fail; for every man must die. His breathing stops, life ends, and in a moment all he planned for himself is ended. But happy is the man who has the God of Jacob as his helper, whose hope is in the Lord his God - the God who made both earth and heaven, the seas and everything in them (Psalms 146:3-6 LB).

Calling Upon God
I want you to trust me in your times of trouble, so I can rescue you, and you can give me glory (Psalms 50:15 LB).

Not as Evil Men
But God says to evil men: Recite my laws no longer, and stop claiming my promises, for you have refused my discipline, disregarding my laws (Psalms 50:16 LB).

But Believing
But when you ask him, be sure that you really expect him to tell you, for a doubtful mind will be as unsettled as a wave of the sea that is driven and tossed by the wind; and every decision you then make will be uncertain, as you turn first this way, and then that. If you don't ask with faith, don't expect the Lord to give you any solid answer (James 1:6-8 LB).

Having Wisdom and Understanding
The man who knows right from wrong and has good judgment and common sense is happier than the man who is immensely rich! (Proverbs 3:13 LB).

Faith

Chapter 3

How do we find this help and happiness that makes life so worthwhile? Let's be specific. How do we apply faith to the everyday problems we have mentioned? As I told you, I thought I was living a good Christian life, but there was no power there for changing things. I had prayed very hard for help and had not found it. But then my life changed and I began to have God's help. The difference was because I did not have faith. This was pointed out to me in a scripture that directly follows the one which tells us to ask for wisdom:

> But when you ask him, be sure that you really expect him to tell you, for a doubtful mind will be as unsettled as a wave of the sea that is driven and tossed by the wind; and every decision you then make will be uncertain, as you turn first this way, and then that. If you don't ask with FAITH, don't expect the Lord to give you any solid answer (James 1:6-8).

I had prayed but I had doubted God's power each time I tried to plan and figure out and manipulate events into solving my problems. That was one reason my prayers weren't answered. That was one reason why it took so long!

The exciting thought about all of this is that even though your problem with unanswered prayer may not be the same as mine was, God can help you understand what YOURS is, if you have faith. And if your trouble is the same as mine was, you will be amazed at the results when you give up your own "self-planning." I've seen this power quite a lot in the lives of women in class, but only in the women who have given up their own figuring out, who have placed their total and complete faith in God to work things out. As I look around I can still see so many Christians who do as the sign in front of a church said, "...they ask God to guide them, then they grab the steering wheel." But when you reach the point of need where you admit that you can't do it alone—as I did—then God can step in.

A good way to begin exercising complete dependence upon God's power and help is to talk each little thing over with Him. Little by little you can completely let go of your life. It's hard in the beginning because we can't change overnight. But if you will let Him, God will come in and guide you. Begin by inserting this one line into each prayer you say. "Dear God, please help me to completely depend on your power to take care of my life." Then every time you feel tempted to push, nag, complain, arrange, or plan anything which has to do with something you have asked God to handle, stop and pray that short prayer. Remind yourself that YOU MUST STOP INTERFERING BEFORE YOU CAN RECEIVE GOD'S HELP. Then continue in all areas of your life to use the prayer asking for wisdom. "Dear God, help me to understand more. What else can I do?" You will find answers to this prayer again and again. They may be painful but the results are certainly worthwhile. And all of the ladies who have been in our classes would certainly say AMEN to that.

Complete dependence upon God continues when you realize the wealth of help that is available in God's Holy Word. Turn to the Bible for help. Through it God can speak directly to you. The scriptures tell us, "The whole Bible was given to us by inspiration from God and is useful to teach us what is true and to make us realize what is wrong in our lives; it straightens us out and helps us do what is right. It is God's way of making us well prepared at every point, fully equipped to do good to everyone (2 Timothy 3:16, 17 LB). So begin a study of God's Word, praying as you read. Pray that you will understand what you read. Ask for the wisdom to see what God wants, rather than what you want. It depends on YOUR VIEW what sight you see. If you look for God's will the scriptures will make total sense. If you look for your will as I had for many years, they will be hard to understand or accept as guidelines for your life.

The scriptures tell us that unless we are fruitful we do not belong to the vine—we are dead branches and will be pruned away. So we have to produce fruit! If we want to influence someone for Christ and produce fruit we can look at the scriptures which explain how to do that. My husband wasn't a Christian so I read and re-read 1 Peter 3:1 which says "Wives, fit in with your husband's plans; for then if they refuse to listen when you talk to them about the Lord, they will be won by your respectful, pure behavior. Your GODLY LIVES will speak to them better than any words" (LB). Therefore if we aren't producing fruit we do not have the godly lives which are speaking to people about Christ. Does your behavior speak "for" or "against" Christ? I had read this scripture many times, but finally I began to understand what it means. It means your husband (or anyone else) knows you are a Christian by the way you act, not because you have told someone you are a Christian, BUT BECAUSE YOU ACT LIKE ONE.

As Matthew 5:14-16 tells us, "You are the world's light - a city on a hill, glowing in the night for all to see. Don't hide your light! Let it shine for all; let your good deeds glow for all to see, so that they will praise your heavenly Father" (LB).

Your light and my light glows at other people. They see Christ in the reflection if we are shining in the right way. And oh how people need to see Christ in our actions toward them. Especially ladies, at home! Our good deeds should begin at home and then can radiate from that center out into the world. If your husband isn't a Christian you know that you need to be shining oh so brightly at home.

But if you are like me, you will need to change some things before you will show a likeness of Jesus' love to others. The very heart of Christian doctrine is that it is ourselves that we must change. We have been told that we must cast the beam from our own eye first and then we will more clearly see the mote which is in our brothers (Matthew 7:5). The seven years that I waited and prayed were years that I stayed the same. I didn't show Christ to anyone because of various bad attitudes, selfishness, and frustrations. I really needed to change. And what a blessing it is to want to influence someone else. What a motivation it gives us. We might never strive to reach higher, we might never try to attain a perfection in love if we didn't see our serious deficit in the area of spreading the good news.

And having a godly life is important. A good illustration of how important our example is, can be shown in the answers I received from ladies who answered a questionnaire I gave them. The women who answered the questionnaires and had husbands **who had already become Christians after their marriage,** said it wouldn't take very long for women to bring their husbands to Christ if the wives were good examples. One lady said it didn't take very long for her husband to become a Christian after they were married. She said that with prayer and God's help it only took ten months. Apparently she had already found the answer to removing the barrier of "self" and showing Christ to her husband through her own example in every part of her life. I hope you will agree that prayer is definitely important toward bringing anyone to Christ, but only when the women who are praying show Christ's love in their own lives in such a way that Christianity becomes a wonderful thing to the person involved.

Make Christianity something appealing in their lives or they will remain uninterested. Our minds are like computers, receiving messages all the time. I once heard that we receive 12,000 messages each day. We don't consciously think about these messages coming into our brain, but they do. They cause us to reach conclusions. We decide what brand of soap to buy, where to take our vacation, and what toys to buy for a gift. Decisions about Christianity come in the same way. Messages received from you cause others to reach conclusions about the value of your religion. So when you act unhappy, nag, complain, or respond to others in unloving ways you are giving them wrong messages about God's love. No one really understands why he feels the way he does about God, but deep inside each of us there is a decision. Of course, background and upbringing cause many of our beliefs, but you have the opportunity to change someone else's beliefs by your actions. Suppose someone had really received the wrong messages about Christianity up to the point where they met you. You don't want to add to the wrong messages, do you?

Be a loving, forgiving, understanding person. That's the way we are treated by God. So that's the way we must treat others if we are to reflect God. Remember the story of Philip and the eunich? Do you suppose that the eunich would have been blessed by Philip's knowledge of the scriptures if Philip's attitude had been bad? Wouldn't that be like going into the grocery and asking the butcher how that roast is? He'd tell you it was fine but when you saw it quite moldy, you would know the truth. The message would go into your unconscious mind not to trust that man. Maybe you would never trust any butcher again, because the words he said did not match what you saw.

Let's be more personal for a moment. How can a man see that Christ could love him even though he is imperfect, if his own wife doesn't love him when he makes mistakes? How can anyone think God can forgive when you don't forgive them? How about God's mercy—can anyone see it if you don't show it to them?

Perhaps we can't see ourselves clearly. We can't see the real image we project. I remember vividly when Bill told me, "You don't really hear what you say, do you?" Well, we don't always SEE the way we are either. We can't get a good understanding of the reflection we give unless we back off and get a look from a distance. This isn't easy to do, but try it this way. Go with me to the sky, pretend we are birds flying along together. We come to your home and stop, hovering outside the window. We are watching you and all of the action that is taking place with your husband, with your children, with your visitors. Would we see a happy Christian? A happy marriage? Would we see you treating your family as Christ would if he were in your body? Would we see you telling your neighbor it's alright that their daughter cursed you out? Would we see you as a demonstrator of God's care by your own dependence on Him to help you with problems? Would we see you ready and able to express a reason for the hope that is within you? Would we see you radiating Christ so much that other people would just have to see what they had been missing?

If your husband isn't a Christian I must ask you to pay particular thought to this - you are the closest person to him. The burden rests on you to show Christ to him. Do everything you can to make your husband's choice clear. Each day he goes out into the world. He sees what the world has to offer: position, wealth, power, gaity, and having a good time. And since God does not force us to choose Him it will be up to you to **show** your husband (show, not tell) that God offers so much more. Freedom of choice is important to God. Very clearly,

He gave Jesus the right to pass His suffering (John 10:18). And He is giving your husband the choice of passing by the greatest thing in heaven or earth. But what kind of choice is it when one side doesn't look good to him at all? To many men, Christianity means a kind of strait jacket where you don't laugh and you aren't happy. Christians are just waiting for death. Why choose it? And often a man's spiritual death comes because no one provided the clear choices. No one ever began the battle with Satan for his soul. Read Ecclesiastes 2:1-26. It tells us that worldly pleasures are a happiness that is fleeting and momentary, a striving for the wind. The devil tries to hide that fact. But with God's help and your godly life, when the times come that the world's happiness begins to look thin (and it will) then you will prove that the choice of a spiritual life is filled with more blessings and joys—now.

Life is a ladder and growth and maturity come in a day by day and step by step process. Although we realize we must climb that ladder for our own sake and for the sake of others, it is hard, often impossible, to change ourself so that each day becomes a better day than the one before. We each need to show Christ to others but we have so much we need, too. I wanted to be a better person, but I wasn't. There were other women who had the strength and courage to lead exemplery lives but I wasn't one of them. If I was successful in one way I was a miserable failure in another. Partially this was because I didn't take the scripture Philippians 4:13 seriously. It says, ". . . for I can do everything God asks me to with the help of Christ who gives me the strength and power." And I was like everyone else; so often we depend on God only in cases of emergency. We believe that God put us here and left us. He expects us to do the best WE can. WE should work and worry, think and plan what WE must do in OUR lives, every step of the way. When extreme problems come we feel we can call on Him to help us. Otherwise we shouldn't bother Him with such things as small problems within our job, getting along with our neighbors, understanding our family, etc. He has said that He knows when a sparrow falls and how many hairs we have on our head (Matthew 10:29,30), but we still feel He is too busy to be concerned about our everyday problems.

I know He isn't too busy to help. I was a frustrated, angry, often depressed, and usually irritable person. Cigarettes and food sustained me. Even if your problems are different than mine, it doesn't matter because God can help you. He can help you BETTER reflect the love and joy of Christ as you go to Him in prayer, as you search the Bible, and as you trust Him every minute. Today I have not touched a cigarette for 7½ years. I am a happy wife and mother, and a happy Christian. Many things have worked together to change me. I am better not because of any ability I have but because God is so wondrously able to give strength and power. Each day is filled with the wonder of His power, available as if it were at our fingertips.

Let God help! Begin in a very definite way. You can do this by inserting this one sentence into every prayer you say! "Help me to do what YOU want me to do, Lord." And as you pray this prayer, picture in your mind you are walking through a cool stream. You are walking along kicking up the silt that lies on the bottom. Then you stop and stand very quietly and watch the dirt settle back to the bottom. The clear stream swirling around your ankles is like your life when it is in God's hands. He can clear the silt from your life if you will really depend on Him. As Hebrews 4:16 says, "So let us come boldly to the very throne of God and stay there to receive his mercy and to find grace to help us in our times of need" (LB).

Even as you continue praying the one line prayers that I have mentioned, when one particular problem arises and you want specific help with it, ask God for specific help. Outline the problem as you see it. Mention exactly what you need. Tell God that you understand He will naturally override your request if it would be more beneficial to do so. But as you ask him for specific help picture in your mind a loose leaf notebook. In this notebook are pages of different problems. Now mentally tear out the page that holds the problem you have prayed about. Imagine yourself crumbling the page into a ball and pitching it into the wastecan. Then try to put it out of your mind. FORGET ABOUT IT. This will take some determination for it will creep back into your mind again and again. But each time it does, form the same mental picture and throw the problem away. You will also find it helpful to simply tell Satan, who is bringing this back to your mind, that God can take care of it and that you command him in God's name to leave you alone. Then wait in peace for God to help you. Always remembering that some problems take time to be taken care of. So call upon patience as you would when you are dealing with a small child by remembering that next year the child will be different and so will the problem. Of course, it will not take a year or even a day for some problems to be solved. You will see very fast results on some points but on others you will very definitely have to wait patiently. Just be certain that while you are waiting patiently you are not interfering with God's power by trying to work out the answers yourself.

Work on all of your problems in the same way. After one problem, one page, has been taken care of by prayer, tear out another and another—praying each time. Eventually you will have the confidence to tear out all of the pages at one time. You can even throw the book away because you aren't going to take care of problems any more—God is. When something appears in your life that you need help with, pray about it, and then forget it. You will be able to do this because past experience will have shown you that God can handle everything just fine. This sounds like I believe it's easy, and it isn't. At first it will take almost more determination than you can muster, especially if you are short on faith as I was. Just remember that each time you try to solve something yourself you are showing a lack of faith. Then God can't help you.

Others can be silently impressed with Christianity just by seeing how you don't worry. And you can also now tell them about how God is helping you. After you have built up your confidence in God's power, and have found the abundance He gives, I hope you will remember this story! Some time ago, my children both in school, I went back to work. The schedule was difficult and many short cuts went into making our lives less hectic. While out shopping one evening I noticed a wig sale. I was earning some money now, I rationalized, so I bought a wig. It was beautiful, long, and dramatically attractive. It did something for me. I really enjoyed wearing it and one day not too long after its purchase, I wore it to work. A lady at the next desk didn't recognize me. I excitedly explained that I had found a sale and since my own hair was short I thought a change would be nice. I told how easy it was to take care of, how convenient and economical. I was exhuberant in my joy over having that wig. Three days later the same lady came through the front door and I didn't recognize her. She was wearing a new wig. She had gone to the sale and had found everything I had told her was true. We often express our joy over a new friend, a gift received, or perhaps a new automobile but how often do we express our excitement over Christ? Would some people rush out to the "sale" and see if what we had told them was true? Would your husband, your neighbor, your friend? Would they know how excited you are about God and how he takes care of your life? Matthew 10:32 tells us that "whoever then will acknowledge me before men I will acknowledge him before my Father in heaven . . ." (NEB). So be open about how God is affecting your life. Don't overdo what you might feel about his help; just be sure to express your joy out loud. And don't expect any reaction from others; just know that you have fed a message into their subconscious mind for Christ. You have planted a seed. You have begun to pass it on.

PASS IT ON

It only takes a spark,
To get a fire going;
And soon all those around,
Can warm up in its glowing.
That's how it is with God's love,
Once you've experienced it;
You spread His love to everyone;
You want to pass it on.

What a wondrous time is spring
When all the trees are budding.
The birds begin to sing;
The flowers start their blooming.
That's how it is with God's love,
Once you've experienced it;
You want to sing;
It's fresh like spring;
You want to pass it on.

I wish for you, my friend
This happiness that I've found.
You can depend on Him.
It matters not where you're bound.
I'll shout it from the mountain top;
I want my world to know.
The Lord of Love has come to me;
I want to pass it on.

I'll shout it from the mountain top;
I want my world to know
The Lord of Love has come to me;
I want to pass it on.

The greatest happiness of all is giving God to someone else. But because of our own incapabilities we know that we are inadequate. But do you recall the stories of how Jesus fed the multitude with only a few loaves of bread and some fish? Your life and my life are like that bread and fish— inadequate for the job at hand. Yet when we hand ourselves into the hands of the Master we become ample for feeding others. Remember, there was even much left over. Baskets and baskets of left-over food. As Christian women we can tell others the good news, and still have much left over for the other tasks that God sets before us.

FAITH IS:

A Happening
Then he touched their eyes (blind men) and said, "Because of your faith it will happen" (Matthew 9:29 LB).

A Way to Live
For it was through reading the Scripture that I came to realize that I could never find God's favor by trying - and failing - to obey the laws. I came to realize that acceptance with God comes by believing in Christ (Galatians 2:19 LB).

Belief in Christ
Yet faith comes from listening to this Good News - the Good News about Christ (Romans 10:17 LB).

Realizing God Is In Charge
We toss the coin, but it is the Lord who controls the decision (Proverbs 16:33 LB).

Trusting Against the Facts
So, when God told Abraham that he would give him a son who would have many descendants and become a great nation, Abraham believed God even though such a promise just couldn't come to pass! And because his faith was strong, he didn't worry about the fact that he was too old to be a father, at the age of one hundred, and that Sarah his wife, at ninety, was also much too old to have a baby. But Abraham never doubted. He believed God, for his faith and trust grew ever stronger, and he praised God for this blessing even before it happened. He was completely sure that God was well able to do anything he promised (Romans 4:18-21 LB).

Believing in God
... Anything is possible if you have faith (Mark 9:23 LB).

Boldness to Come to God
So let us come boldly to the very throne of God and stay there to receive his mercy and to find grace to help us in our times of need (Hebrews 4:16 LB).

Obey His Will

Not all who sound religious are really godly people. They may refer to me as "Lord," but still won't get to heaven. For the decisive question is whether they obey my Father in heaven (Matthew 7:21 LB).

Trust the Scriptures

The whole Bible was given to us by inspiration from God and is useful to teach us what is true and to make us realize what is wrong in our lives; it straightens us out and helps us do what is right (2 Timothy 3:16 LB).

Trust the Holy Spirit

And in the same way - by our faith - the Holy Spirit helps us with our daily problems and in our praying. For we don't even know what we should pray for, nor how to pray as we should; but the Holy Spirit prays for us with such feeling that it cannot be expressed in words (Romans 8:26 LB).

Prayer

Chapter 4

> I pray that you will begin to understand
> how incredibly great his power is to help
> those who believe him. It is that same
> mighty power that raised Christ from the
> dead and seated him in the place of honor
> at God's right hand in heaven, far, far
> above any other king or ruler or dictator
> or leader (Ephesians 1:19-21 LB).

Trying to understand God's power and the part it plays in our lives is difficult. His power is so great we can't really explain it or even thoroughly understand it—but we know it surrounds us. We have the written Word, the Bible; we have the Holy Spirit; and we have the power of prayer. All of these things play extremely important parts in our life. Another thing is certain also. There are hindrances to the flow of power from God to us. This has no doubt been evidenced in all of our lives at one time or another. In classes we have shared the many times that help was needed but (apparently) was not received. But we have also reached some conclusions about that. In my life and in the lives of class members we find that the real weakness and lack of power comes from an obstructed prayer life.

Prayer has been defined as a conversation between you and God. This conversation has many values, one of which is to help you receive God's help in your life. And just as a telephone conversation must be carried across telephone lines, so our prayers need to be carried across lines. But we find the lines are plugged up and the prayers aren't getting through. I believe this is because we have a fence around us. I'd like you to think about God in this way: He is a never ending spirit which reaches from the beginning to the end of everything. Where you are, He is. His spirit is composed of, among other things, total and unending energy. This energy and power is ready and waiting to be used for His loved ones IF THEY REMOVE THE FENCE WHICH SURROUNDS THEM.

We have a fence, a negative force field you might call it, which surrounds us sometimes. We need to remove it, piece by piece if necessary, to allow God's power to reach us. God does not detain His force of power from reaching us. WE DO. There are many sections of that fence which have to be removed for a complete and total flow of power across the lines. You may not be able to remove all of the pieces at once. I don't know about you, but it took me quite a while to learn about all of the negative pieces in my life. In our classes we have often remarked about how the power is apparently more available when we pray together in a group. And I can't help but believe it is not only because we have been told that "where two or three are gathered, Christ is there" also, but that it is because in a group the negative pieces in my life are overruled by the positive pieces in someone else's life. This is only a theory, of course. Nevertheless we have seen the proof in our lives that as the negative pieces are removed from an individual's life the prayer power increases.

So, if you will, let's look at the positive things which need to be replacing the negative pieces:

(1) Have Faith! Open your mind humbly to God in complete trust. You can't ask God to help and be asking with faith unless you act like you believe. I remember my grandfather telling about his trip to a country church where he was to speak to the congregation. The appointment had been made and grandpa was well and able to make the trip but he didn't have the money for the fare. As I heard the story, grandpa told grandma not to worry, said a little prayer, and went to the bus station. There a woman came to him and paid him some money she had owed him. It was enough to cover the bus fare with some left over. Grandpa calmly said thank you to the lady, and thank you to the Lord, and climbed on the bus. Now if we don't have faith as he did, we will find ourselves standing empty-handed. The Bible says, "Because of your faith it will happen." The meanings of the Greek word faith are: reliance upon, dependence on, adherence to, and

trusting in. Read 1 Samuel 1:10-28 and Daniel 6:23. These are good examples of God's answer to prayer. They will strengthen your faith.

(2) Think positively! When you pray, form a picture in your mind of the difference in your life when your prayer is answered. See yourself with the problem taken care of. Allow your mind to focus sharply on the fact that God is right this moment working on it for you. Do not allow your mind to think of failure because no matter how your prayer is answered it will be in the right way and in the best way for everyone involved. Therefore no matter how it might seem to you or to everyone else, God is taking care of the problem.

(3) Ask!

> You haven't tried this before, (but begin now). Ask, using my name, and you will receive, and your cup of joy will overflow (John 16:24 LB).

> Ask, and you will be given what you ask for. Seek, and you will find. Knock, and the door will be opened. For everyone who asks, receives. Anyone who seeks, finds. If only you will knock, the door will open. If a child asks his father for a loaf of bread, will he be given a stone instead? If he asks for fish, will he be given a poisonous snake? Of course not! And if you hardhearted, sinful men know how to give good gifts to your children, won't your Father in heaven even more certainly give good gifts to those who ask him for them? (Matthew 7:7-11 LB).

> For the Father himself loves you dearly because you love me and believe that I came from the Father (John 16:27 LB).

These verses tell us that God loves us and will help us if we ask him. But there are so many times when we throw up our hands in hopelessness because WE can't figure out a solution. The power is there but we block it by not asking.

(4) Want! Many are the times that we ask for something but we do not really want what we are asking for. We can't sit

back quietly and expect Him to do it all. We should constantly put our energies into life as we continue praying. We will show by our actions that we WANT to be strengthened, WANT to remain strong, WANT to raise Christian children, and WANT God's help. Do your best to reach these goals you are praying about. For example—do your best to raise your children as Christians by not keeping them away from other Christian children and from Bible school, because if we keep them away that would be telling God we don't REALLY WANT Christian children. How many times do we pray that God will guide our children's lives and that He will watch over them but then we let them go right out into the worst possible situations. We just want to leave it all to God. And that's not what "wanting" is all about.

> The earnest prayer of a righteous man has great power and wonderful results (James 5:16b LB).

But are we acting in our lives as if we "earnestly" WANT what we are praying for? Actions speak louder to God than words.

(5)   Be Courageous! We don't pray many times because we feel so imperfect. Our past mistakes loom up in front of us and cause us to miss many chances to pray because we feel so inadequate. But the Bible doesn't teach that we must be perfect before God will answer our prayers. Perfection is impossible to attain anyway. The children came home from camp one year with a good story about this.

> A man had a dream. In this dream he saw God, who handed him an enormous piece of chalk, larger than he was. God said, "You must climb this ladder and when you get to the top you will find a blackboard. Put a small mark on the blackboard for each bad thing you have done."
> So the man began climbing the ladder. He felt that he was very near the top when suddenly someone stepped on his hand. It was another man, a leader in the church, coming back down the ladder. The church leader said, "Don't tell anyone but I have to go down for another piece of chalk."

And of course, we are all like that church leader. No one of us, when measured against God's goodness, could even begin to attain perfection. The Bible says that God alone is truly good (Matthew 19:17). In the same chapter we find the story of the rich man who was told to give what he had to the poor and that he would attain perfection. The scriptures go on to tell us that we will find perfection in LOVE if we will only follow Jesus. We need, therefore, to give up anything that stands in the path between us and Jesus. That is the only perfection that will allow the power of God to work in our lives. "Elijah was as completely human as we are and yet when he prayed earnestly that no rain would fall, none fell for the next three and one half years." So with courage, knowing our inadequacy, we can go to him in prayer with the complete confidence that He will help.

(6) Be serious about following Jesus. Have the right attitude and goals and you will receive more power in your praying. A young lady I knew asked me, "Why doesn't God answer my prayers?" She had prayed a great deal, many times with tears streaming down her face, yet it seemed her smallest prayers weren't answered. Now I don't mean to judge this young woman, but everyone around her knew that her attitude was bad. She was selfish and thoughtless of other people. She went day after day trying to get what she could out of other people. She would establish relationships only because they would be beneficial to her needs. And when she wasn't pushing other people into doing things her way (which wasn't often), she was telling everyone how sad her life was. And many of us knew that in doing that she was "setting them up" for the next favor she would need. When I looked at this young lady I was seeing the same attitude I had seen in myself and in others. And I was seeing the same result. Miserable people without God's love and power, in their lives. Miserable people who alienate their friends, their family, their children, and apparently God. Isaiah 1:11-16 gives us a glimpse into God's feelings when we live selfishly.

> I am sick of your sacrifices. Don't bring me any more of them. I don't want your fat rams; I don't want to see the blood from your offerings. Who wants your sacrifices when you have no sorrow for your sins? The incense you bring me is a stench in my nostrils. Your holy celebrations of

the new moon and the Sabbath, and your special days for fasting—even your most pious meetings—all are frauds! I want nothing more to do with them. From now on, when you pray with your hands stretched out to heaven, I won't look or listen. Even though you make many prayers, I will not hear, for your hands are those of murderers; they are covered with the blood of your innocent victims. Oh, wash yourselves! Be clean! Let me no longer see you doing all these wicked things; quit your evil ways. Learn to do good, to be fair and to help the poor, the fatherless, and widows (LB).

Thankfully, we know God is merciful when we turn from our unloving, sinful ways into a different direction of living for God. Of course, we all fall short of this mark, but if our goal is right God will hear our prayers; if it is not he will not. The young girl's attitude was selfish. Her prayers weren't answered because she lived for herself, not for the Lord.

If I gave everything I have to poor people, and if I were burned alive for preaching the Gospel but didn't love others, it would be of no value whatever (1 Corinthians 13:3 LB).

Although Cornelius was not a Christian, his generous gifts to the poor (his generous heart) came up as a sacrifice to God and were remembered to him. God answered his prayers and sent Ananias to teach him.

(7) Forgive! Prayers are definitely hindered when we do not show love, concern, and understanding for each other (1 Peter 3:7). But we find this difficult when it comes to the application in our own lives. Forgiveness of others becomes hard when we are the ones who have been hurt. But Jesus told us that we must forgive others or we won't be forgiven. And if we are not forgiven it is fairly apparent that our prayers have no power.

If you only have faith in God—this is the absolute truth—you can say to this Mount of Olives, "Rise up and fall into the Mediterranean," and your command will be obeyed. All that's required is

that you really believe and have no doubt! Listen
to me! You can pray for ANYTHING, and IF
YOU BELIEVE, you have it; it's yours! BUT
WHEN YOU ARE PRAYING, FIRST FORGIVE
ANYONE YOU ARE HOLDING A GRUDGE
AGAINST, SO THAT YOUR FATHER IN
HEAVEN WILL FORGIVE YOU YOUR SINS
TOO (Mark 11:22,25 LB).

How can we expect God to forgive us if we do not forgive
our brothers, sisters, children, husband, neighbors, friends.
God does not tell us to straighten out others. He says to let it
drop—FORGIVE IT (Mark 11:25). I have found that a good
way to forget something that has settled on my mind is to
think real hard to find something just the opposite about the
person you can't forgive. For example, if a lady is spreading
gossip about you, forget the gossip—let it drop—and look for
some good thing in her favor. Perhaps she is a fine mother, or
a good cook, or she is especially nice to strangers. Whatever
you can find that is to her advantage, think about this thing.
Consider that God knows her faults and her good points,
surely He is happy about the way she takes care of her
children, is friendly to strangers, etc. If God loves her, how
can I do anything else? There is a poem that tells how much
we would have to know before we could judge someone else.
We would have to know their life from the beginning to the
present, how they were raised, what problems they had had,
what they had learned or not learned, how much they had
been loved or not loved, etc. Surely I cannot know these things
about anyone, my closest friend or my dreaded enemy. God is
the only one that knows everything about us and He loves us
anyway. He also has reserved the right to do any judging that
needs to be done. He specifically tells us to forgive it and to let
it drop. If you have any resentments against others, let them
drop right now. If you need to apologize for an unforgiving
attitude please do that right now.

(8) Confess! Humble yourself to admit your mistakes to
God. We have learned that our attitude should be based on
love—total love, a complete unwavering love for God and for
others. We have learned that we should not direct our efforts
toward our own self. So if we have not been doing these
things we need to find forgiveness before God will hear our
prayer. We must confess our sins.

He would not have listened if I had not confessed my sins. But he listened! He heard my prayer! He paid attention to it! Blessed be God who didn't turn away when I was praying, and didn't refuse me his kindness and love (Psalms 66:18-20 LB).

Also read Proverbs 15:29; 28:9, Lamentations 3:44, Jeremiah 7:16; 11:14; 14:11, Proverbs 12:22. Remember, Peter denied Christ. Christ said to him, "So when you have repented and turned to me again, strengthen and build up the faith of your brothers" (Luke 22:32 LB).

(9) Question your true feelings about God as seen in your life. The disciples asked Jesus how they should pray. He gave them an example which we call, "The Lord's Prayer." In this example, Jesus tells us to pray with certain attitudes, among them reverence. Reverence is shown in our prayers, by the way we address the Father and acknowledge His greatness. Lack of reverence is shown in our lives by dressing immodestly, missing worship services, and by generally treating God as if He were not so great. We thank God in our prayers for many things, but do we live our lives as if we are really thankful? If we treat our family with no respect or concern, if we contribute to the pollution of our environment, if we do not share our abundance with others less fortunate— are we really thankful for our families, our land, our money? Look to your heart as you pray to see if your heart matches your prayers. God knows what we feel. And we know our children appreciate what we do for them, but how much better it is to hear them say it and to see them acting as if they really feel that way. So also it must please God to not only see us acting as if we appreciate and revere him, but to hear us say those kinds of words as a part of our prayer.

This has been a chapter of many negatives. There are many negative pieces of fence that have to be removed before we can experience the tremendous positive influence of God in our lives. But it is so wonderful to have God's help in our lives that cutting away the bad so the good can come in barely hurts at all. What a relationship we can have with our Father in heaven if we are willing to be the kind of child he wants us to be!

Then we can talk with God at any time and see wondrous things happen. He will walk with us every minute of the day—while we clean house, iron, sew, shop, or go to our job. The switchboard doesn't close at certain times of the day either. A friend once told me about her "washing dishes" prayer, "ironing board" prayer, and "gardening" prayer. And up to that time I had not experienced the great and wonderful help from God through prayer so I had no need for different prayer times. But later I really appreciated knowing that it is perfectly proper and consistent with God's will that we pray "without ceasing." Kneeling beside a rose bush with the fresh dirt in our hands can stimulate a prayer of thanksgiving for the bountiful earth. While washing I am reminded how grateful I am that I can take care of my family.

Use prayer for many things. Pray in emergency. Psalms 50:15 says, "I want you to trust me in your times of trouble so I can rescue you, and you can give me glory" (LB). What a wonderful opportunity we have then to tell others about our great God. Pray in a group (Matthew 18:19,20). It's a wonderful way to find a stronger power. We have seen so much of this in our classes. Pray to be released from temptation. By virtue of Christ's own temptation, he is able to help those who are exposed to it (Hebrews 4:15,16). When you find something that wants to have control over your life—pray about it. And if you have a habit that you don't really want to be rid of—pray that you will WANT to be free of it. God will answer that prayer and every prayer with specific help. He will furnish your mind with reasons and new thinking. He will give you opportunities for change that would not normally have occurred.

So part of prayer becomes our ability to listen to God's answers. God replies constantly, but we do not always want to hear Him. Christ prayed three times saying, "Thy Will Be Done," Father (Matthew 26:39-44). We know that, as a man, Christ didn't want to suffer the pain and anguish of the crucifixion; yet, as he prayed, "Thy Will Be Done," he was affirming his belief that God was completely trustworthy. He knew that God could take all things into consideration; things that are above a man's feelings or understanding, and still answer in the best possible way. So we too should affirm the same reliance in God to decide what is best knowing that Luke

12:32, says "and fear not, for it is His pleasure to give us the kingdom."

As a godly woman once said, "I have found that God and I together can do much more than I was able to even imagine myself."

> Don't be weary in prayer; keep at it; watch for
> God's answers and remember to be thankful
> when they come... (Colossians 4:2 LB).

PRAYER IS:

Powerful

Now glory be to God who by his mighty power at work within us is able to do far more than we would ever dare to ask or even dream of - infinitely beyond our highest prayers, desires, thoughts, or hopes (Ephesians 3:20 LB).

Coupled With Faith

You can get anything - anything you ask for in prayer - if you believe (Matthew 21:22 LB).

Conversation With God - He Has Great Understanding

How great he is! His power is absolute! His understanding is UNLIMITED (Psalms 147:5 LB).

Through Christ

Ask, using my name, and you will receive, and your cup of joy will overflow...for the Father himself loves you dearly because you love me and believe that I came from the Father (John 16: 24,27 LB).

Useless For The Godless

But what hope has the godless when God cuts him off and takes away his life? Will God listen to his cry when trouble comes upon him? For he does not delight himself in the Almighty or pay attention to God except in times of crisis (Job 27:8-10 LB).

To Be Earnest

For night and day we pray on and on for you, asking God to let us see you again, to fill up any little cracks there may yet be in your faith (1 Thessalonians 3:10 LB).

With Thanksgiving

Don't be weary in prayer; keep at it; watch for God's answers and remember to be thankful when they come (Colossians 4:2 LB).

Not Meaningless Repetition

Don't recite the same prayer over and over as the heathen do, who think prayers are answered only by repeating them again and again (Matthew 6:7 LB).

From the Forgiving Heart to the One Who Forgave So Much
But when you are praying, first forgive anyone you are
holding a grudge against, so that your Father in heaven
will forgive you your sins too (Mark 11:25 LB).

For Others
Now take seven young bulls and seven rams and go to my
servant Job and offer a burnt offering for yourselves;
and my servant Job will pray for you, and I will accept
his prayer on your behalf, and won't destroy you as I
should because of your sin (Job 42:8 LB).

Where Two or More Gather
I also tell you this - if two of you agree down here on earth
concerning anything you ask for, my Father in heaven
will do it for you (Matthew 18:19,20 LB).

Peace
Don't worry about anything; instead, pray about everything; tell God your needs and don't forget to thank him
for his answers. If you do this you will experience God's
peace . . . (Phillippians 4:6,7a LB).

Who Are You?

Chapter 5

Whether you are looking for God's help so you will be a happy Christian or because you want to influence someone else toward Christ, you need to know who you are. Otherwise you can't really use everything else that we are learning about. Therefore the next two chapters will be devoted to an inward look at the "self."

Each one of us, however complex and mysterious, are unique. Unique means having no like or equal, being the only one of its kind, rare, unusual, unmatched, single. In other words—YOU ARE SPECIAL. No one in the world is exactly like you. God knows this. He loves YOU. We are told in the stories about the prodigal son and the lost sheep, that God cares about individuals. He sent His Son to die for individuals. I hope you can do what I had to do. And that is—to take a look at yourself as if it were a view from God.

Some years ago there was a program on television which had, as part of the story, a simple test. A woman was asked by her psychiatrist to write exactly what she believed were the most important ingredients in her life. She was to list them in order as she rated their importance. The most important was number one, next important was number two, and so on.

How do you see the different sections of your life? You are a woman, a feminine human being; you are a wife, a person who is part of a marriage; you are a Christian, one of God's children. You may be a mother, a nurse, a teacher, a chemist, a writer, a thinker, an employee, an employer, a secretary, a business woman, a friend, or whatever else you see yourself. Use the space below and list what you feel are the major parts of your life, at this time.

_____   _____

_____   _____

_____   _____

Now after completing this list, rearrange the items, in the space below, into a numerical order according to their importance in your life. Take plenty of time to consider each position. Place them in their proper order by deciding what is RIGHT NOW, first, second, and third in your life.

Don't try to figure out what **should** be on your list or what should be in the first, second, or third place. Just list them as you really believe they are, right now, in your life. Be completely truthful, because then you will have an insight into yourself.

1. _____   2. _____   3. _____
  (most important)   (next important)   (next important)

After you have completed this exercise you should, in some ways, be able to see yourself as God sees you.

Next, I want you to look at yourself in another way. Do you see yourself as a mixture of good and bad? Or do you feel as I did, that the majority of your good points are outshadowed by the bad points? How would you rate yourself on a scale of 1 to 10? _____ (10 is high.) Take the time to put a number in, that you feel best fits your value to God and to others.

There is no one really good except Jesus. We are all so imperfect when compared to His love. It is only through the goodness of Christ dying for us that we can even talk to the Father now. No one of us deserves this blessing, or the future blessing of living with Him. So no one of us can rate ourselves too high. Neither should we rate ourselves too low. Because God sees us through the eyes of love. And loves sees the good not the bad.

Are you satisfied with yourself? I know you would like to be perfect in God's sight. We all want to be strong and full of righteousness for the Lord. We'd like to be able to smile at life's problems knowing they will pass, feel a sense of peace when a loved one dies knowing he will go to be with Him, stop worrying about how our children will grow up or how we'll be taken care of when we're old. We would like to be able to take food to others when we're too busy, keep out of town company in our homes when we can't, love a boy and girl who smell of unwashed clothes and marijuana; but we just don't. We would like to have happiness and joy in our marriage and good communication with our children. Sometimes we don't though! We would like to accomplish a lot in this world, and in our neighborhood, and in our own hearts. But sometimes we can't.

Do you have peace and contentment in your heart? Are you cheerful and pleasant most of the time? Do other people enjoy being with you? Are you satisfied with what you have? Have you had anyone find Jesus because of you? Have you come full circle from finding God's happiness yourself to where you now pass it on to others? I remember vividly when our minister asked me to go give a Bible study with another lady. I thought of every excuse in the book. And was I relieved when he accepted my no. That was when I realized that something was wrong.

I was not strong in my faith. I had no strength. I had nothing to give anyone else. I also lacked inner happiness. How do you rate yourself? One, Ten, or somewhere in between? Well, I'd like to emphasize that you can change that rating. I did. With God's help. And you can too. You can be a better example to your husband, your children, your neighbors, and your fellow Christians. You can find a special joy and peace; filled with a new happiness because you have discovered that with God's help we can do and become more than we could dream.

How is this accomplished? By taking a long, hard look at ourselves. Just as we have been doing. Understanding exactly who we are and where we stand should help us see what occupies the majority of our thoughts, what we devote the most time and energy to, and what we receive the most happiness and satisfaction from.

When I took the test at the beginning of this chapter I began to see that Christ was not number one in my life. I knew He should be. Sure I was a Christian, I attended church regularly, but I did not live for Christ. And if we aren't living for Him, we aren't plugged into the power. A fan won't work unless it's plugged into the power and neither will we.

Take a look at the things that make up our lives: motherhood, a job, hobbies, etc. All of these things satisfy our need. This is a law of human nature. We are all uncompromisingly searching for happiness and fulfillment of our OWN needs. This is the basic urge inside our bodies. This urge can be called our search for growth, happiness, and satisfaction. As our hunger pangs tell us we need food, so our pangs of need tell us to search for satisfaction. We search for love. We want to feel good and to accomplish. This is natural. We want to be strong, full of faith and righteousness. We want total joy and peace. We want others to see Christ in us. Consider for a moment the little flower just beginning to grow. It sticks its head out of the soil searching for the sun. Its roots spread out looking for the water and food which are in the soil. And it grows.

We stick our heads out looking for the things we need to fill and satisfy us, to make us grow, but we stretch in the wrong direction. We try to find happiness by turning back into ourselves as the source of our strength. And if the flower did that it would be contorted and bent. It would be very weak.

When we live to our own satisfaction Christ is not first in our lives. We are making ourselves the source and are ignoring the true Sun and Water of life. And Satan likes this process very much. He helps us develop it. We are tricked by the little happinesses we see. We are fooled by smooth talk at times (Colossians 2:4). We can go to a party and join the gaity, thereby forgetting our problems. We can look at healthy children and cover up the fact that they might get sick or die. We can look at ourselves in good health and forget that our bodies will grow old. We can look to the world to take care of us and our needs for as long as it takes, until we come to that point when the world fails us. The smooth trickery flows on and on until we come face to face with the problems, the death, the bad health. Then we need strength from God and we have none. Living our lives without God's help is like cake batter without a pan. A cake has many ingredients that go into it; just as we do, but without a pan to hold the batter, the cake will be runny and weak. If we don't let God furnish our needs, control our lives, we will be like the batter without the pan - WE WILL RUN ALL OVER THE PLACE. Our growth will be stunted and twisted. We will not be happy or worthwhile.

The result could bring us into mental institutions and psychiatrists offices. I found this article in a church bulletin. It was written by a lady who found this out the hard way.

> I was a victim of Me-I disease, commonly known as mental illness. This is one of the most devastating diseases known to man. It cripples the mind, the body and the soul. I know from experience how tragic this disease can be because I traveled the dark and agonizing road of mental illness for four years. After many visits to a psychiatrist, I realized only God could help me overcome my illness. I remembered Christ's words when He said, "Come to me all you who labor and are heavy laden and I will give you rest" (Matthew 11:28). The day I determined to accept His invitation and submit my will to God's will produced a peace and rest to my mind, body and heart that I had never known before. I am truly convinced there is one simple cure for mental illness and that is service; service to God, to others, then to self. Serving others has helped me to overcome my illness more than any factor involved in my therapy . . . Ruth Adkins.

2 Timothy 1:7 tells us that God has not given us a spirit of fear but a spirit of power and love and **a sound mind**.

There is no way we can grow into strong, happy people with the peace of Christ unless we stretch our heads toward Him who supplies all that we need.

> And now just as you trusted Christ to save you trust him, too, for each day's problems; live in vital union with him. Let your roots grow down into him and draw up nourishment from him. See that you go on growing in the Lord, and become

strong and vigorous in the truth you were
taught. Let your lives overflow with joy and
thanksgiving for all he has done. Don't let others
spoil your faith and joy with their philosophies,
their wrong and shallow answers built on men's
thoughts and ideas, instead of on what Christ has
said (Colossians 2:6-8 LB).

The difference between proper growth and improper
growth, between fear and courage, between plugging into the
power or shriveling up, is WHO SETS THE GUIDELINES:
YOU OR GOD? Is God's name on your mailbox - in large bold
letters? Are you living according to your will or God's will?
The scriptures describe people who decide against God's will:

People will be lovers of self and (utterly)
self-centered, lovers of money and aroused by an
inordinate (greedy) desire for wealth, proud and
arrogant and contemptious boasters . . . (They
will be) lovers of sensual pleasures and vain
amusements more than and rather than lovers of
God. For (although) they **hold a form of piety
[true religion] they deny and reject and are
strangers to the power of it**" (2 Timothy 3:2, 4b, 5
AV).

Just as Christ had the opportunity to choose (John 10:18) we
also have the chance to make a decision. Which way will you
live your life?

Are you a Christian first or do you allow your own desires to
come before God's will in your life? If you do as I had done,
using excuse after excuse to keep from doing what God has
told you to, then you are following your will, not His. "Woman
without spiritual wings is a dismal worm. There is no odor so
bad," Thoreau says, "as that which arises from goodness
tainted." Yet if we do not follow God's will COMPLETELY,
we are "goodness tainted."

But if we forget self we will find we can accomplish more
than we ever thought possible. If we really want to do God's
will because we believe with an intense belief that God's will is
the very best that can ever happen to anyone, we can set goals

for ourselves beyond our wildest imagination. There are stories the world over about God working on a design in the lives of people. And I have felt that working in my life as I have written about my inadequacies and my failures hoping that they would glorify God. If you could have only known me in the past you would know that it is not my normal nature to tell "all" or even to reveal myself slightly to my best friends. But as I began to let go of myself and let God guide me, I found that for all of my shyness and fear, God had an answer. I had never dreamed of being a writer and as far as I knew had no special aptitudes toward writing—yet here I write about many things so others will understand and enjoy God's love. I am doing this because the events that lead up to my writing this book were unquestionable. That doesn't mean I didn't question, because I did. But the answers remained constant, guiding me to do something that has been a joy. God can see much more than we, and He can supply the help we need where we need it. I needed so much when I began this book, and through God's power everything has been supplied. There have been classes, books, articles and the insights of friends that have completed sections in a remarkable way. You see - ALL we need comes from Him, who CAN and WILL help us if we are totally committed to **His will.** Whatever it may be.

The following steps will tell you how you can attain a complete giving up of SELF-WILL. I pray that you will take them as I did and decide right now to apply them in your daily life.

1. Decide that even if you are miserable, unhappy, and full of needs, you will follow God's will. Decide as David did in Psalms 48:14.

For this great God is our God forever and ever. He will be our guide until we die (LB).

2. Expect God to help you grow through the passing of time by guiding your life and its experiences. Don't expect to be changed all at once. But know that:

The lot is cast into the lap, but the decision is wholly of the Lord - even the events (that seem accidental) are really ordered by Him (Proverbs 16:33 AV).

3.   Please promise not to interfere with the help God can supply.

    a.   Don't shrug off the food He gives; read and study His Word.

    b.   Don't pull the clouds around your shoulders shutting out His warmth by using negative and pessimistic behavior.

    c.   Accept the water necessary for life by determining to be with and around other Christians every chance you have.

    d.   Believe He does work through others and would like to use your hands.

4.   Search yourself and pray fervently about your probems, expectantly awaiting the relief He has promised from your heavy yolk (Matthew 11:28).

5.   Promise to turn away from evil. Don't embrace it in any way.

(Turning away from evil) shall be a health to your nerves and sinews, and marrow and moistening to your bones (Proverbs 3:8 AV).

6.   Remember to earnestly ask for help with the sins you do not want to give up yet, knowing He will provide you with the help you need to change your desires.

So also the Lord can rescue you and me from the temptations that surround us. . . (2 Peter 2:9 LB).

7.   Trust Him to bring you to a full maturity so you will know true happiness and joy.

If we do these things we will find that the old characteristics of self-will are gone. No longer will other things be number one in our life. God can take over and make us different, according to His WILL.

      The kingdom of God is not just talking, it is living by God's power (1 Corinthians 4:20 LB).

And make no mistake about which choice you are making. You cannot go part one way and part the other. You can't follow God's will some of the time and your own will the rest of the time. This is wasted time. Each moment, each hour, each day spent trying to use the wrong method to find happiness is wasted time. One day, when you need great strength, you may look back regrettably, wishing you had the time to do it over again. There is no waste when you are with God.

WITH GOD

To talk with God no breath is lost; Talk on
To walk with God no strength is lost; Walk on
To toil with God no time is lost; Toil on
Little is much, if God is in it;
Man's busiest day not worth God's minute.
Much is little everywhere
If God the business doth not share.
So work with God, then nothing's lost
Who works with Him does well and the most.

(From **Christian Woman Magazine**, July-Aug. 1971.
R. B. Sweet Publishing Co.)

WHO ARE YOU?

Don't Try to Understand Everything

I know that you can do anything and that no one can stop you. You ask who it is who has so foolishly denied your providence. It is I. I was talking about things I knew nothing about and did not understand, things far too wonderful for me (Job 42:1-3 LB).

Seek His Will First

And he will give them (food, clothing, care) to you if you give him first place in your life and live as he wants you to (Matthew 6:33 LB).

Not the World's

Don't copy the behavior and customs of this world, but be a new and different person with a fresh newness in all you do and think. Then you will learn from your own experience how his ways will really satisfy you. As God's messenger I give each of you God's warning: Be honest in your estimate of yourselves, measuring your value by how much faith God has given you (Romans 12:2,3 LB).

As God Wills

He went forward a little, and fell face downward on the ground, and prayed, "My Father! If it is possible, let this cup be taken away from me. But I want your will, not mine" (Matthew 26:39 LB).

Obey Him

The one who obeys me is the one who loves me; and because he loves me, my Father will love him; and I will too, and I will reveal myself to him (John 14:21 LB).

Now - Not Later

Another of his disciples said, "Sir, when my father is dead, then I will follow you." But Jesus told him, "Follow me now!" (Matthew 8:21,22a LB).

Turn To Him

(That, by the way, is what baptism pictures for us: In baptism we show that we have been saved from death and doom by the resurrection of Christ; not because our bodies are washed clean by the water, but because in being baptized **we are turning to God** and asking him to cleanse our HEARTS from sin) (1 Peter 3:21 LB).

Change Your Attitude

Now change your mind and attitude to God and turn to him so he can cleanse away your sins and send you wonderful times of refreshment from the presence of the Lord (Acts 3:19 LB).

Trust Him Completely

And now just as you trusted Christ to save you, trust him, too, for each day's problems; live in vital union with him. Let your roots grow down into him and draw up nourishment from him. See that you go on growing in the Lord, and become strong and vigorous in the truth you were taught. Let your lives overflow with joy and thanksgiving for all he has done. Don't let others spoil your faith and joy with their philosophies, their wrong and shallow answers built on men's thoughts and ideas, instead of on what Christ has said (Colossians 2:6-8 LB).

t's Only Me!

Chapter 6

The next section that we want to look at is our "inner self." Our inner self requires attention before we can be certain that God cares for us and will really help us. Our inner self has to be cared for before we can ever experience "inner happiness." This inner happiness is not love, or having love but is something that is quite independent of anyone else. Lack of inner happiness has caused divorces, battered children and suicide. It keeps you and I from reaching the potential that God intended us to have.

This potential is described in "the perfect woman" verses, Proverbs 31:10-31. This woman was busy, happy, and radiated her concern for others in every deed she did. She had inner happiness and because she did, she could be the woman she was. Whenever I read these verses about this perfect woman I really want to throw up my hands and say that I can never come anywhere near doing everything she did. But if you look closely I believe you will find as I did that she was able to care for others because she cared for herself also. She was not idle, discontent or full of self pity. She functioned as God intends women to function because she had no walls built inside herself that hindered her work. She knew her reason for being.

> As each of you has received a gift (a particular spiritual talent, a gracious divine endowment), employ it for one another as (befits) good trustees of God's many-sided grace - faithful stewards of the extremely diverse (powers and gifts granted to Christians by) unmerited favor (1 Peter 4:10 AV).

We are to use our talents for others.   But we can't if we are unhappy and miserable.   We need to be fixed up inside before we can reach out to others, get involved in their problems, feel deep concern for the poor and unfortunate, help people in the dark find the Light. If you have found these things hard to do it may be that you are in need of a little UNSELFISH concern for yourself. So look ahead with me at some of the things that have been problems for me and for other ladies who have come to our classes.

The worst problem is GUILT.   We all have had days, months, years that have gone past, where guilt lies.   No matter who we are we all have past guilt to reckon with. Many times we have been unlike God.   There are times we can't even remember and there are times we wish we could forget. There may be sins we have not yet repented of. These sins present an unresolved wall between us and God.   This wall remains as long as we do not confess our sins to God.

And even though we may have confessed these sins to God in the past, if we have continued to make the same mistakes over and over again, we have not really repented of them. When we are really sorry we will change our mind and our purpose, turn around and walk differently.   Then God can forgive us.

> Now change your mind and attitude to God and
> turn to Him so He can cleanse away your sins and
> send you wonderful times of refreshment from
> the presence of the Lord (Acts 3:19 LB).

The wall also remains when we have asked God to forgive us, changed the way we were acting, but didn't really accept God's forgiveness.   We feel unworthy of his mercy and know that common justice demands that God condemn us for our actions.   But remember - WE ALL ARE UNWORTHY.

There is no one who can be good enough, work hard enough, pray enough, worship enough or do anything else enough to earn the right to enter heaven. God tells us how much He loved us (John 3:16) and that the gift He gives is free (Romans 5:18). The price He paid for us is all out of proportion to what we can do to repay; all we have to do is accept.   So don't listen when Satan whispers in your ear, "You can't be good enough to suit God," or "How could He love YOU?" The same thing happened in the garden. God said one thing and the serpent said another thing.

We can not listen to all of the inner feelings we have; we want to listen only to the ones that agree with God's Word, only the ones that are consistent with God's nature. Read your Bible and see if you can find a man that God looked at and said, "This is SUCH A GOOD MAN, I love him better than anyone else!" Only Christ was good and He died for you, offering you complete forgiveness, if you will only accept it. Irregardless of our feelings we have the gift of total erasure available if we will only accept it. The blackboard is wiped clean.

> No dear brothers, I am still not all I should be but
> I am bringing all my energies to bear on this one
> thing: Forgetting the past and looking forward
> to what lies ahead. . . (Philippians 3:13 LB).

I believe that God has offered us the opportunity to soothe our guilt in another way, by offering us the wisdom to understand why we have sinned. There are things in our nature that cause us to act the way we do. This is not a rationalization but is rather a real· way to deal with the inability to accept forgiveness. I believe God will help you if you pray this kind of prayer, "Lord, help me to see what it is in my nature that I need to change with your help. Help me to understand and increase my dependence on You."

> Happy - blessed, fortunate (enviable) - is the man
> who finds skillful and godly wisdom, and the man
> who gets understanding—drawing it forth (from
> God's word and life's experiences) (Proverbs
> 3:13 AV).

If we refuse to accept God's forgiveness we are holding Christ up on the cross again. And we will also be wasting the rest of our lives. Today is the first day of the rest of it, you know, so live it free of guilt, wrapped in the love of God.

As freedom from guilt is a gift of God, so is our life situation a gift from God. But for some reason we often find it hard to accept our life situation. The perfect woman "was not discontent." She accepted what God had given her and was happy with it. And we are commanded to do the same (1 Corinthians 7:17). So if you are rich or poor, sick or well, if you must work to make ends meet, if you are not beautiful, if you have lost your family, it is essential that you accept your situation. Not only because it is a command of God but because good mental health, inner happiness and peace all begin with an acceptance of one's own life.

This has been a special problem for women whose husbands aren't Christians. They must realize that their husbands won't act as a Christian would. This is natural - accept it. His feelings, opinions, and understandings are also valid - accept them. Don't ridicule his beliefs, don't argue with him about his opinions, and most of all don't treat him as if he really doesn't feel the way he says he does. Accept also the hardships that accompany being married to someone who isn't a Christian. You will have to display more courage and stamina than women who are married to Christians. And they will never understand just how hard it is to come to church without him unless they have been through it. Even then, it is easy to forget. But you will understand and accept that also. Continue to attend church without him but don't attempt to take part in each and every little thing that comes along, leaving him alone a lot. Accept the fact that you can't do the same things you could do if he were a Christian. Then you can be content.

We can all be content if we will humble ourselves before God's will. Job is our prime example of this acceptance. He had faith in God. Of course, having this kind of humble faith isn't always easy. It requires that we trust God even when it is very difficult. This kind of acceptance means several things; actions will be different, words will be spoken without anger or intolerance, and love will begin to sprout stronger and stronger. You will stop reacting to things you don't like. Instead you will pray more short quiet prayers and you will show your acceptance by smiling a lot.

Recovering from guilt and accepting one's situation are important to gaining inner happiness, but just as important is your ability to treat yourself fairly. Don't expect to give more than you can. When your children are small, don't try to accomplish as much as women whose children are in school all day. When your husband works long days and isn't able to be home a lot, don't be discontent, but look for things to do that will keep you from being idle.   You will find a tremendous blessing in helping others.   Then you will find you are revitalized.   As wives and mothers we have a lot to give to our families, but we need to find the opportunities to rest, to relax, and to rebuild our strength. Accept these needs and see that you have the time to rest.   When the children are young it is hard to find time to rest.   Each of us will find it in a different spot.   Some might get a baby sitter for an afternoon a month and go shopping. Others may sleep half an hour longer in the morning just to have the peace and quiet. Perhaps you like to take a book and hide in the bathroom for awhile, simply because it's the only room with a lock on the door.   But whatever method you devise, don't give up the building of your inner reserves.

There is no better way to build inner reserve than reading the Bible and praying. We have often shared in the classes our praying and studying times with our families or by ourself. Some women like to rise early and pray and study then. Others like to wait until the day is over.   However you can fit this into your household schedule, don't neglect this important part of your inner needs.

I believe that another way to achieve success in finding inner happiness will be our ability to think positively. If you can think positively you will have more power in your life. Success will flow toward you.   You will achieve positive results. On the other hand, people who think negatively and experience many "bad days" often make those days bad because they have already convinced themselves that nothing will go right that day.

"With God's Help" classes have helped many ladies realize that they were thinking negatively.   They found they were saying "I can't" entirely too much and not enough of "with God's help" I can.

Do you know if you are a positive thinker or not?   This story may help you decide.

There was a man who so angered his king, that the king sentenced him to death.   The man begged to have another chance, so the king said, "Very well, you may live, if within the space of one year you can make this horse fly." Elated, the man ran to tell his friend. The friend said, "What's the use, you can't make a horse fly!" But the man looked at his problem in a positive way and said he thought he had an excellent chance - in fact he could think of three chances he had to get out of the death sentence. See if you are a positive thinker! What chances can you think of?

3. The king could die.
2. The horse could die, giving him more time.
1. The king could change his mind.

Be a positive thinker! Train your mind by placing positive thoughts into it and you will find life changing for you. You see, thoughts are a habit and you can change your thought pattern by placing different thoughts into your mind. Remember your successes and forget your failures. Look at failures only long enough to see if they present a certain pattern of doing the same type of thing over and over. Then look at your successes. Think about them and relish them. Eventually you will find this process becoming easier and easier.

Apply this positive thinking to your own abilities. Lack of confidence is one of the worst problems that we have to deal with today. God made us in His image. Think about this for a moment. If we are made in His image, were we made to be unsuccessful? Look around you at the people you know who have ability. We are told that God is no respector of persons. So you must have ability also. Certainly God made us to be successful, not to fail. He has given us each some talent which we are to use. We might not know what it is - but with God's help we can find it.

We can find it if we are not afraid. Everywhere we go we encounter people who are afraid. They don't believe that they can handle life and since they don't want to be called failures, they actually accept much much less in life than they need to. Some people are actually so afraid of life and failure that they can't admit they are afraid. Fear can get so large, like Topsy, "it just grows and grows" until we have the one out of four Americans who will at sometime in his or her life suffer such serious mental illness as to require hospitalization or intensive clinic or office treatment.

Mental illness means that a person can't assume the responsibilities that a person of his or her age, intellect, and physical capacity should assume. Mental illness means that we are not emotionally stable, we are not mature of character, we do not have the strength or ability to stand up under the stresses of living without undue or persistent symptoms, either physical or psychological. Mental illness may come from causes that we can't deal with here, such as senility and retardation due to physical causes, illnesses of the body enzymes that cause malfunction of the brain, etc. The mental illness which we must speak of here, which should never occur among Christians whose faith is grounded in God, is the inability to cope with life due to lack of strength and confidence in God. This kind of mental illness is called neurosis, or a nervousness, a sense of being afraid and anxious and depressed about the problems we face. This, when it continues into symptoms that impair our capacity to carry on our own personal business of living, is the kind of illness which shows our lack of confidence in God.

This is a natural occurence among people who have not learned to place their hope for life in God. If we have not learned how to do this and have therefore lived without God's help, when the large problems arise we will not know how to turn them over to God also.

There is only one way to do this, and in the process put your inner self at peace; TRUST EVERYTHING TO GOD. When something begins to worry you, make a special effort to stop whatever you are doing and pray about it. Pray that you will find a solution, or that the thing you are worrying about will not occur. Always end your prayer with the affirmed belief that God's overall concern is for good, so that you will accept His Will in everything. Therefore whatever answer comes from your prayer, you will know that it is in God's will because you have turned it over to him. The only thing that inhibits this process is if you do not let go of it - then the answer may not be in God's will at all.

I have found that I can completely turn a worry over to God if I mentally picture the problem in my head. Then I imagine myself opening a door in my head and sweeping the worry outside. Then I close the door and lock it tight. Then I make myself physically relax while I continue praying and I picture the problem as being resolved. And I have found that since worry inhibits the useful process of our minds, turning a worry over to God often allows me to see a solution that I would not have seen otherwise. I do believe that the devil is secretly happy when we worry, so let's make him very unhappy. Make a concentrated effort to change the thought patterns you have established, little by little.

I'm sure that the strong women we know, some in the public eye, get to be strong because they have dealt with life's experiences and fears, one by one, little by little. As with Alcoholics Anonymous, a day at a time is the only way to handle things. You shouldn't look ahead and try to see what will happen. You shouldn't look behind and say "Since such and such happened to me, it'll probably get worse" (negative thinking). You need to deal with each day by placing that day in God's hands. And when you hold God's hand, you have a hand full of strength. Use that handful and He will give you another and another and another. He will guide, protect, strengthen and help you grow. This is real confidence, real courage, and real destruction of fear and worry, deep down inside of your inner self. I know that I will have problems in life that I could not handle at this point but I also know that if I turn myself into God's hands now, He will prepare me for whatever lies ahead. Then I will be able to thank God in the midst of pain and distress (Colossians 1:11). The only other choice is to meet these future events by myself, all alone. Truth makes me admit that I can not. And I pray that truth will help you admit that without God's very real and present help, you cannot either (1 Peter 5:5,6; Psalms 46:1; Jeremiah 10:23,24).

So all of these preceding points are important to finding inner happiness, but there is one yet to look at before we can truly be released from our inner bondage. I have saved it for last because I hope by this time you will have recognized some of the earlier problems as being problems in your life. If you have then you can more easily look at this last point.

Accept your total self. As with each snowflake that falls and with each fingerprint that exists, there are no two of us alike anywhere in the world. We have a combination of needs, problems, and talents that makes us totally unique and unlike anyone else. And we need to accept that total self just as we are, right now. We need to accept our past mistakes, our present situation in life, our guilt, our lack of confidence, and especially our abilities. In other words - YOU ARE YOU!

I remember Bill's mother telling a story that I feel tells us how we ought to feel about ourselves. She said that one night when she and Bill's dad were sleeping, she woke up with a start because he was leaning over her with his fist doubled up. He was punching her on the arm, over and over. "Tommy, Tommy, you're hurting me," she said, trying to get up. He was sound asleep and dreaming, but he smiled and said, "Be quiet, Momma, IT'S ONLY ME," as he continued to punch her.

So also, we need to look at life with the same attitude. With God's help, we will punch at it, and when it hollers back, we can smile and say, "It's only me." I have to deal with you as only I can, because I am me. No one else would or could live exactly as I will. I am only responsible for whether or not I allow God to use ME as best He can.

Like yourself! Surely you are a person who can and will be molded by God, and you AREN'T FINISHED YET. But you can be happy with who you are so far. God will take it from here. But like who you are right now.

Then and only then can you begin to look for the talent that God has given you to be used for others. Don't bury that talent - use it! And if you haven't found it yet, search diligently for it. Try to remember the things you used to do while you were growing up. This can be a clue. Perhaps you drew fashions for paper dolls, or molded clay into shapes, or whittled on a bar of soap; maybe you wrote detective stories or helped mom cook; perhaps you liked to paint or work with animals. Any such enjoyable feature of your younger life could very well be a clue to the hidden talents you haven't seen yet. Pray that God will help you find out what He wants you to do. He'll let you know - believe me! He'll help you find that talent and you won't have to disturb your vital position as a wife, mother, or Christian, in order to use that ability.

Then reach out to others with it. Some ladies I know have started a preschool class for children. Others sew for orphans. Still others teach young girls how to cook and sew, making presents for children in the hospitals and for shut-ins. Dorcas (Acts 9:36) was famous for her acts of charity and service. She was a Christian who knew the joy that comes from doing the work that God wants us to do. Then as complete and fulfilled women we can each find a happiness that is hard to explain. But as one lady said recently, "I have found such happiness in my relationship with God and my service to others, that even if my husband never becomes a Christian, I can say in all honesty, I am happy." This pretty well sums it all up. I hope you will find this happiness also.

I AM ME

Valuable

Look at the birds! They don't worry about what to eat - they don't need to sow or reap or store up food - for your heavenly Father feeds them. And you are far more valuable to him than they are (Matthew 6:26 LB).

Lifted Up

If you will humble yourselves under the mighty hand of God, in his good time he will lift you up (1 Peter 5:6 LB).

Valuable

And the very hairs of your head are all numbered. So don't worry! You are more valuable to him than many sparrows (Matthew 10:30 LB).

Sinful

If we say that we have no sin, we are only fooling ourselves, and refusing to accept the truth. But if we confess our sins to him, he can be depended on to forgive us and to cleanse us from every wrong. (And it is perfectly proper for God to do this for us because Christ died to wash away our sins.) If we claim we have not sinned, we are lying and calling God a liar, for he says we have sinned (1 John 1:8-10 LB).

Special

God has given each of you some special abilities; be sure to use them to help each other, passing on to others God's many kinds of blessings (1 Peter 4:10 LB).

All That Christ Wants Me To Be

I don't mean to say I am perfect. I haven't learned all I should even yet, but I keep working toward that day when I will finally be all that Christ saved me for and wants me to be. No, dear brothers, I am still not all I should be but I am bringing all my energies to bear on this one thing: Forgetting the past and looking forward to what lies ahead... (Philippians 3:12,13 LB).

Doing For Others

So ever since we first heard about you we have kept on praying and asking God to help you understand what he wants you to do; asking him to make you wise about spiritual things; and asking that the way you live will always please the Lord and honor him, so that you will always be doing good, kind things for others, while all the time you are learning to know God better and better (Colossians 1:9,10 LB).

# I'm A Woman

Chapter 7

When we took the test in Chapter 5 about the important parts of our life we found that we are Christians first; it is necessary to follow this at some point by an understanding that we are WOMEN second. Just as being a Christian affects our total life, so does being a woman. It colors everything we are and everything we do.

And I needed to question just how much being a woman is supposed to affect my Christianity. The only way I know to do that, is to take a look at the "women's liberation" movement as it pertains to me, a Christian woman. I know that the woman's liberation movement began because women realized that being a female caused us to be treated differently. They saw how each facet of their daily experience related to their womanhood and they knew that in many cases, due to traditional treatment, their life was a "mere" existence, a pitiful emptiness. They weren't happy with the way they were treated because they were women.

So they began searching for special rights and freedoms as INDIVIDUALS rather than continuing to experience the stifling and smothering they had previously received because they were women. And perhaps this had to happen if only because throughout past history woman has been treated as if she were inferior. She has been enslaved and degraded in many cases. As a woman I know that if I were to go out into the world and become regularly employed at a job, my pay would not equal that of a man doing the same job. That is changing some now, but it is still not as it should be. I am aware that if I were single or divorced, it would be extremely difficult to establish a credit background sufficient to purchase a home or other large item. As a woman I also know that there are many wives who experience degrading treatment from their husbands. Since time began, I know there have been periods in history, in some countries, where women were only recognized by the men as a sex symbol and nothing else. There are still some areas in the world where women are treated inhumanly.

We all want to see changes in these areas. And because of these bad situations, the women's liberation movement can make some very valid points in favor of the work they are doing, especially in the category of "single" women. A woman has the right to be treated fairly. The women in the Bible were cherished, protected, and understood by Christ. They were protected by God's laws and given prominence through the birth of Jesus. Women were shown to be essential and important by the repeated reference that the Church was the "bride" of Christ. Women were treated with understanding and sympathy by Christ (Luke 10:38-42; Matthew 5:27-32). Laws were given to protect her weakness and her freedom (Deuteronomy 21:10-14; 22:13; 22:28). She was spoken of with respect. Christ performed the first miracle for a woman.

So we, as women, hope to have the same kind of treatment today. If tradition has caused us to miss out on some of the treatment we would like to have, should we abolish tradition as the women's liberation group seems to want? I believe that instead, we should look at God's guidelines for women. And I have found in my own life, that by following God's commands to women, I have also been partaker in all of the glory that comes from being a woman. Everything that is really important is given back when we give up our will to God's will.

There are many women who need to find the glory that can be theirs. They are miserable and unhappy women. Eloise is a good example of the bored and frustrated mother. She is always tired. She frequently serves TV dinners at the evening meal, uses a lot of safety pins to mend the children's clothes and very seldom cleans house. Her lack of accomplishments are not because she has no time, but because the highlight of her day is getting the mail and watching the 2:00 p.m. soap opera. After the soap opera is over, she spends a lot of time on the telephone, particularly when the children are coming home from school and also while she is fixing dinner. She has a long telephone cord so she can talk and prepare dinner at the same time. She particularly resents being interrupted during these phone calls, although they are really not very important.

Sheila is different. She manages to keep her house clean by frequently inviting company over for dinner. She has learned that, if she knows company is coming, she will get the house clean before they arrive. She complains a lot about the children and picks at her husband. In fact it seems no one ever pleases Sheila, even Sheila. She gets very upset over nothing. A long nap helps her get through the depressing days when she has nothing to look forward to. Frustrations and lack of freedom seem to fill every day.

A woman can wonder, "Is this all there is," as she shops for groceries each week, always buying the same thing, always running out of money. "Is this all there is," she asks, when the trying times come, when the children fail in school and her husband become irritable and grouchy because his job is making him unhappy. "Is this all there is," she asks, when she attends weddings and funerals, but her own life seems to stay the same, suspended in a kind of cage with bars all around - and she can't get out.

She says, "Dear God, these children of mine (I love them dearly), but they are always crying and pulling at my skirt. Sometimes I think I am growing childish myself for lack of adult conversation . . . And as they get older, they begin to expect decisions from me that are difficult because I've been away from the world during these growing up years. CAN I GO TO THE MOVIES, MOM? (Can all movies really be that bad?) When should I begin worrying about the dope problem and the sex problem that I read about? In Junior High? (That young?) Surely the world hasn't changed that much since I was in school, has it? These teenagers need my patience I know. I don't want to alienate them, but I really can't seem to get my mouth to stop talking. Do they really need to rebel that much? . . . My house is empty, they are all gone now, married, in college, and where did all the years go? What do I have to show for them WITHIN MYSELF?"

Many of us feel the same way! We have experienced many of the same feelings and have done the same things. The individual incidents that make up the lives of these ladies are not so bad, in themselves. I have a favorite soap opera that I like to watch. I invite company over knowing that I will have to accomplish more this week than last week. We are women and we have many similarities, but the sum total of our lives should not be waiting for the mailman and taking a nap. Don't let your life be governed by circumstances outside of yourself. Don't be happy and excited just because you were invited to a nice party and then be let down after it is over, because now there is nothing else to look forward to.

Our lives should be challenging and exciting. But many times they aren't. Some of this happens because our lives today aren't made of the same demanding chores that women in past history had. It is no longer necessary to spend hours baking and preparing from "scratch" in order to place a fine dinner on the table. It is no longer necessary to put the curtains on the stretcher in just the right way. Today our work ranges from driving 50 miles to visit friends, to taking the dog to the vet, from helping the children learn to swim, to entertaining the boss and his wife. You've probably read one of those lists that tell about women. We are everything from nurses to secretaries, from accountants to caterers, from seamstress to gardner, from painter to decorator. The problem about all of this complexity is that we feel a different kind of pressure.

Because we are expected to do a lot more in a lot less time, for some women it seems a hopeless battle to try to be everything to everybody. And they end up being nothing to anyone. Again they are caught in a kind of cage, with bars all around, and they can't get out.

There are ways to fight this. Lisa has decided to attend meetings of the local women's lib group. Her husband doesn't like it much but she feels she must find some identity of her own. And in this thinking process she has decided to ignore her heritage as a woman and to search for equality with the men. Others have realized their predicament and are determined to spend as much time as possible away from home. They know that the hours at home somehow fall into a routine of boredom.

"What do you think of women's lib?" One woman asks another in the television commercial as she sticks her head from under the hair dryer. "I'm for anything that will get me out of the house!" another lady answered.

We must get out of the house and run hither and yon, picking up things at the store, visiting friends and keeping busy. Somehow we fill these weekly hours with many activities that overflow and make us late getting home to fix dinner, too busy to take the children to the park, too confused to plan family activities, and too tired to think. We do this to get out of the rut of the house into a stream that forces us to keep moving. We can't stop to rest.

What is the answer? Can we solve these situations? Is there an answer? Suppose the women from Bible times were transported to our city or town and placed in homes to function in today's life. What would they do?

Women haven't changed - only the world around us has changed. We are women today just the same as the women from Bible times. And God hasn't changed. He is the same. His will is the same. His will for women is the same. In doing His will for women, today, we will find the joy in being women that we want so much. Trusting the Father, our Maker, to have plans and purposes in mind for us will bring us challenges and joy. Let us look into the Bible to see what we should do.

To begin this study we need to go back to the creation.

It is not good (sufficient, satisfactory) that the man should be alone; I will make him a helper meet (suitable, adapted, completing for him) (Genesis 2:18 AV).

The first thing I see in this description, is how urgently important women are - or God would not have created us in the first place. We are needed as HELPERS. We are needed to COMPLETE the man.

The Bible continues as it says that woman was created in a special way from part of the man removed from him by God (Genesis 2:21,22). So we will always carry that part around with us and as part of the man was taken from him, he will never be complete without the woman helping him. The two shall become one (Genesis 2:24). And as I see this, in marriage, because of this dependence both the man and the

woman need each other. Neither can or should be sufficient
unto himself. Now they need to turn to each other for help.
This then is the ideal situation. But how do we put this into
practice.

First I believe we need to accept what our Creator has said.
Now by accepting what God has said about women and
deciding to follow God's outline for womanhood, we are
realizing that we are needed for our own special attributes.
We are partner-helpers, completing for the man, essential,
important, and needed for our own abilities. We are needed
because we have feminine characteristics that contribute to
life and to the men. Man does not have these characteristics
and therefore cannot contribute what we can to the world.
Who but a woman could teach a child about the beauty of a
cotton dandelion blown into the wind or a fluffy cloud that
looks like an ice cream cone? Who else could help a man hang
onto his sanity in this world of high pressures? Who else could
fulfill the job of helping your family in its suffering and
problems as well as YOU? With God's help, of course!

The frustrated and bored women who have no pleasure in
their undemanding lives, have not yet accepted the full responsibility that belongs to this job of being a helper. They
have not admitted that they, as women, are vital to the world
in their own way. The women who run back and forth with
such urgency and fierceness, yet never have the time to touch
the cheek of their child as he comes home from school, have
not accepted the importance of their function in the lives of
everyone around them. Our families need us to "mother" them
and to teach them with a hug and a smile. They need us to care
for them with the needle and thread, with the brownie or cub
scout troop, with planning regular devotional times, and with
caring about their needs.

It is exciting to open our hearts to the needs around us. We
can keep up with the schools and with the neighborhood, with
the candidates and with the people who are in need. We can
soothe the scratches and bandage the wounds. We can be a
helper of many.

Now I introduce and commend to you our sister
Phoebe, a deaconness of the church at Cenchreae,
that you may receive her in the Lord—with a

Christian welcome—as saints (God's people) ought to receive one another. And help her in whatever matter she may require assistance from you, for she has been a HELPER of many including myself—shielding us from suffering (Romans 16:1 AV).

The scriptures that speak of the ideal woman in Proverbs 31:10-31 are beautiful. What a feeling they give. It's like seeing a beautiful picture in its entirety, yet also piece by piece. Each woman is a beautiful picture, a uniquely special picture, made of the many facets of her character. And no matter what makes up your own personal character, you can fit into that picture of a beautiful woman. The beauty that leapt out of the picture painted in Proverbs was the fact that she cared. Her whole day consisted of caring. And she used every ability she had to show that she cared; for her household, for her neighbors, for the community, and for the church.

Christian women need to be concerned about showing concern for others. And we can do this when we have learned about having God's help in our life. Because then we know that God is in charge and we are freed to use ourselves for whatever needs there are. Happiness comes only from accepting the role that God gave us and the responsibilities that go along with it. Only then will we find fulfillment and real freedom.

Many Christian women have asked themselves the same questions that we are trying to answer here. I did. My husband didn't want me to go out at night without him. He didn't want me to leave him overnight to attend a retreat or to go to camp. I felt closed in. I felt a lack of freedom. A recent movie, "The Stepford Wives," depicts how it would be if women were dolls that did exactly what the men wanted and no more. And the men think that this is just great. They would like that, naturally. But there is a middle ground for each family. And that means that the husband gives a little and the wife gives a little. This is all possible if a woman realizes the position that God has given her and accepts it and its limitations. After giving up my own rights and desires I found that God helped give them all back in great quantity.

Making the decisions involved in being a woman will require you and I to simply turn to God for the answer. We know that we can't do everything that needs to be done. We also know that there are some needs we have that really need to be met. There are of course other needs that we can do without until God sees fit to help us receive them at a later time. We are Christians and our communications with Him and His answers to us can assure us that we are doing what He wants us to do. And trusting His goodness, we will accomplish a lot.

I remember one experience in particular. I asked God what I should do about leaving one area of work in the church to go to another area of work. I prayed about it and asked Him to let me know if it was alright for me to quit by sending someone else to take my place. It was only a few days later that a lady came up to me asking about the job with interest. She and a friend ended up taking the job and doing much more than I could have. This has happened a couple of times since then. And each job was taken over and handled by someone who could do a better job. How great He is!

I believe that for many Christian women, the problem of over-involvement looms large. It is extremely difficult to say no if someone asks your help but you feel that you can't handle any more. We must realize that we are not indespensible - God is! Talk each question over with Him. And then rest assured that if you really want to do His will, He will give you an answer.

It is God's will that we are in the position we are in. We need to accept the life that God has given us. Rebekah (Genesis 24:59) was sent to a strange land. She didn't let this disturb her. She accepted the life that God gave her and went on to do her feminine duty - she was kind to others, including her husband Isaac. AND HE LOVED HER!

Part of this position that we need to accept as women rests in our being adaptive and submissive wives. The scriptures teach that wives are to be SUBJECT TO and TO ADAPT THEMSELVES TO their husbands, in everything! This is the life that God has given us. (Oh, but this is a different subject entirely, you say! We want to be helpers and to accomplish a lot in the world using our femininity, but we want to do it OUR WAY.) Yet you know as well as I do, that if we do not study the question of submission, we will not really be accepting our womanhood. Because women have been treated badly in the past, we have an ingrown fear of submission. We feel that if we give a man an inch, he will take a mile. But God's teaching on submission is so much more important than that worry. We must remove our ideas about tradition and simply look at God's plan. The teaching on submission has a pattern. Look at this pattern and you will see much much more.

1. WOMEN be submissive to MEN. We are not to teach or have authority over men in religious assemblies. We are to learn to be quiet and submissive (1 Timothy 2:11-13, 1 Corinthians 14:34, 1 Timothy 2:9).

2. The next part says that WIVES are to be subject to and adapt themselves to their HUSBANDS in everything! (1 Peter 3:1-5, Ephesians 5:22,24; Colossians 3:18).

3. It continues - CHRISTIANS submit to the spiritual guides of the church (Hebrews 13:17).

4. Next, SERVANTS be submissive to MASTERS (1 Peter 2:18).

5. Then, PEOPLE be submissive to AUTHORITIES (Titus 3:1, 1 Peter 2:13-25).

6. Also, ANGELS, AUTHORITIES, POWERS, be submissive to HIM (1 Peter 3:22, James 4:7).

7. Finally, in 1 Corinthians 15:27, the SON HIMSELF will also subject himself to the FATHER, who put ALL THINGS UNDER HIM.

SO THAT GOD MAY BE IN ALL, THAT IS, BE EVERYTHING TO EVERYONE, SUPREME, THE INDWELLING AND CONTROLLING FACTOR OF LIFE.

Isn't this why we are Christians? Because the Father is our master, and controls our lives? Look at this pattern again:

Women under men
Wives under husbands
Christians under spiritual guides of the church

Servants under masters
People under authorities
Angels, authorities, powers, under Him
The Son under the Father

SO, IT IS BEING SUBJECT TO GOD THAT MAKES US SUBJECT TO OUR HUSBANDS. For a husband is head of his wife, just as Christ is head of the church and the wife is in submission to her husband because she loves the Lord. This doesn't mean we are inferior. This doesn't mean that a man functions better or thinks more intelligently than a woman. It simply means that we are placed under the man's responsibility and in accepting that fact we will place our husband in the position of headship, letting him make the CONTROLLING DECISIONS OVER OUR LIVES. As in any rank of command, someone needs to be in charge. Someone has to have the final say. God gave the man that right. And I believe that as this all reflects our being subject to God it is good to again look at our example. Christ submitted Himself to the Father when He died on the cross. And I believe He was telling us, "Look, it's all right, as long as you do what my Father tells you. You can't go wrong. Please don't ignore what I have done by refusing to do what God wants YOU to do."

Women who can't accept this should consider a couple of points. When a woman has had to take over the job of making decisions because she has lost her husband, she finds it much more difficult than she imagined. But many times we think the grass is greener until we step over to the other side. Of course, most of us don't want to make the decisions all the time. We only want to make some of them. And women who try to say, "Wouldn't it be better to do it this way, John?" will find that in many cases the husband will back off and the wife will step into the head position even though she isn't aware she is doing it. But the second point is this - when a wife does this, she is severely wounding a relationship that God has set up. And usually the marriage will end up in the "destruct file." It begins with the husband feeling miserable and it continues as the wife expresses her view more and more. The fuse has been lit and the only way it can be extinguished is for the wife to step completely back from the head position. (More about this in the chapter on marriage.) The woman who is totally dependent and submissive to her husband's will and decisions, and who therefore is practicing acceptance of God's plan, will find real happiness. And the effect of your happiness and your total submissiveness WILL ALLOW your husband to make GOOD decisions. A man will accept the total responsibility and will handle it well if it is given to him freely, with no hint of a desire to control things, on the woman's part. But a woman who is critical and always nagging a man to make certain decisions or to plan a certain way, WILL CAUSE HIM TO MAKE BAD MISTAKES. He will make mistakes that will get worse, not better, because God gave man the rule over the household, but WITHOUT A WOMAN'S CONFIDENCE - A MAN CANNOT RULE.

> A wise woman builds her house, while a foolish woman tears hers down by her own efforts (Proverbs 14:1 LB).

> That kind of deep beauty was seen in the saintly women of old, who trusted God and fitted in with their husbands' plans (1 Peter 3:5 LB).

Great joy will be ours, when we do it God's way! I'm glad I'm a woman. There are times when a yellow buttercup glistening with dew is a quiet voice from God saying, "I love you." There are times when the fluffy clouds floating overhead say, "I'm protecting you." I see these things because I am a woman. And I need these insights to help me be the kind of woman God wants me to be—adapting, submissive, helping others. I do not want to lose the chivalry of men who no longer feel protective over us because we have tried to dominate and control, plan and regulate, figure and map out, the man's world. Then we will have lost our charm, we would become unfeminine, uni-characters, with no tears that speak of hurt and remind men there is gentleness in the world; no soft hair that speaks of giving in - in a world where men have to fight. The hearts of men will not respond as they should. The mutual help and inter-dependence will be gone. We will have lost our special place as women and will be without God's help.

How does your husband see you? Does he see you full of joy through a total appreciation of your nature as a woman - in response to his nature as a man? You are his woman, yet perhaps you find no joy in that. And if that joy is lacking he will know it - just as the children know when mom is tired, just as the Lord knows when we don't really care for him. Your joy has to be real. When it is, your huband becomes something special. He has a woman who is shining because she is his partner-helper and she is dependent and trusting upon him. And your joy comes because you are grateful the burden of complete responsibility has been lifted from your shoulders and he is carrying it. He will feel that and you will find in return, he will try to understand your needs. His admiration of you will increase and he will become more and more interested in what you feel and what you believe. Your relationship will become a delightful thing and you will also have the assurance that it is blessed by God's help every step of the way.

I'M A WOMAN

God's Will For Women

And the women should be the same way, quiet and sensible in manner and clothing. Christian women should be noticed for being kind and good, not for the way they fix their hair or because of their jewels or fancy clothes. Women should listen and learn quietly and humbly.

I never let women teach men or lord it over them. Let them be silent in your church meetings. Why? Because God made Adam first, and afterwards he made Eve. And it was not Adam who was fooled by Satan, but Eve, and sin was the result. So God sent pain and suffering to women when their children are born, but he will save their souls if they trust in him, living quiet, good, and loving lives (1 Timothy 2:9-15 LB).

Women should be silent during the church meetings. They are not to take part in the discussion, for they are subordinate to men as the Scriptures also declare. If they have any questions to ask, let them ask their husbands at home, for it is improper for women to express their opinions in church meetings.

You disagree? And do you think that the knowledge of God's will begins and ends with you Corinthians? Well, you are mistaken! You who claim to have the gift of prophecy or any other special ability from the Holy Spirit should be the first to realize that what I am saying is a commandment from the Lord himself. But if anyone still disagrees - well, we will leave him in his ignorance (1 Corinthians 14:34,38 LB).

Submission

You wives must submit to your husbands' leadership in the same way you submit to the Lord. For a husband is in charge of his wife in the same way Christ is in charge of his body the church. (He gave his very life to take care of it and be its Savior!) So you wives must willingly obey your husbands in everything, just as the church obeys Christ (Ephesians 5:22-24 LB).

Christ is Over All

For the rule and authority over all things has been given to Christ by his Father; except, of course, Christ does not

rule over the Father himself, who gave him this power to
rule (1 Corinthians 15:27 LB).

God Made Us For a Purpose

And the Lord God said, "It isn't good for man to be alone;
I will make a companion for him, a helper suited to his
needs" (Genesis 2:18 LB).

But still there was no proper helper for the man. Then
the Lord God caused the man to fall into a deep sleep,
and took one of his ribs and closed up the place from
which he had removed it, and made the rib into a woman,
and brought her to the man (Genesis 2:20,21 LB).

This explains why a man leaves his father and mother and
is joined to his wife in such a way that the two become
one person (Genesis 2:24 LB).

Fit In With Husband's Plans

Wives, fit in with your husbands' plans; for then if they
refuse to listen when you talk to them about the Lord,
they will be won by your respectful, pure behavior. **Your
godly lives** will speak to them better than any words.
   Don't be concerned about the outward beauty that
depends on jewelry, or beautiful clothes, or hair arrangement. Be beautiful inside, in your hearts, with the lasting
charm of a gentle and quiet spirit which is so precious to
God. That kind of deep beauty was seen in the saintly
women of old, who trusted God and fitted in with their
husbands' plans (1 Peter 3:1-5 LB).

Let Your Light Shine

You are the world's light - a city on a hill, glowing in the
night for all to see (Matthew 5:14 LB).

Be A Good Wife

A worthy wife is her husband's joy and crown; the other
kind corrodes his strength and tears down everything he
does (Proverbs 12:4 LB).

Not Crabby

It is better to live in the corner of an attic than with a
crabby woman in a lovely home (Proverbs 21:9 LB).

Not Cranky

A constant dripping on a rainy day and a cranky woman are much alike! You can no more stop her complaints than you can stop the wind or hold onto anything with oil-slick hands (Proverbs 27:15,16 LB).

REMEMBER — JESUS PERFORMED HIS FIRST MIRACLE FOR A WOMAN

John 2:3-5

# Husband

Chapter 8

The last three chapters have been devoted to women, so now it is only fair that we take a look at your man - your husband. Genesis 2:7, tells us that God made him from the dust of the ground (but you and I know that a few frogs, snails, and puppy dog tails got mixed in by accident). Then God breathed into his nostrils the breath of life. And man became a living person. He was placed in the garden and God told him to be responsible for it (Genesis 2:15). Then woman was made and the man was made responsible for her also (Genesis 3:16).

When you were married, your husband took on his shoulders the responsibility of you and the children you will have, for the rest of his life. He will be responsible when you are sick, when the children are sick, when he doesn't have a job, when he has a job he hates, when he is sick, when you need a place to live, when the children need to go to college, when the grandparents become old and ill, FOR THE REST OF HIS LIFE. He has chosen not to accept the single life with extra money to spend and no responsibilities, because he believes the best life is being married. Since he has chosen you, he obviously believes that the best life is being married to you. So in choosing you and taking on the responsibility of caring for you, he also realizes that he will HAVE TO WORK (Genesis 3:19) many years to take care of not only himself but of his family. As head of the home, your husband is not assuming a privilege as much as he is assuming a LARGE RESPONSIBILITY. He begins married life with a load that no wife can fully understand.

This man has NEEDS also, and many women don't understand a man's needs. You may try to help him carry his load, not understanding that he has THE INNER NEED and the inner resources to be responsible for his family. God made him that way. When the wife attempts to take part of the weight of this burden from him, he feels its weight even more, because his inner need, his male ego, is being damaged. It is important that a wife recognize her husband's needs including his need to be the responsible head of the family.

A man's requirements are different from a woman's. His ego is that of a man, and is not the same as a woman's. His temperament is different and so is the way he tackles a problem. He looks at it from a different angle than a woman does. Many times his solution will look totally wrong to you. But you must realize that he is looking at the problem in a different way than you would. His relationship to the home is also different than yours. A woman is the center of the home, she holds it together and is primarily responsible for its smooth functioning. A man is the backbone, the provider. He goes out into the world and works to give the home what it needs. He gives his strength by his presence, his attitude and his love. And a man needs his home to be a comfort to him when he comes back to it each day. He has spent hours working for his responsibilities and when he comes into the door he needs to receive comfort from it. My mother used to say, "Wait until dad has had his supper before you tell him your problem." And I have always tried to do this whenever possible. Make your home a place where your husband wants to come. He needs that very much.

He is deeply involved in his work. One of the questions I asked women in class discussion is, "Why do you feel so many men are uninterested in the church (as opposed to women)?" A large portion of the women who answer say that they believe it is because a man finds fulfillment in his job. And that's true - they do. They can become more and more engrossed in their jobs, finding comfort in the fact that they are accomplishing a lot. They can find comfort in having more money and comfort in having power, but a man's comfort SHOULD COME from YOU and from the atmosphere you provide at home. A man's fulfillment should come from his share of the responsibilities involved in raising his children and in encouraging his wife. But many times a man cannot assume these responsibilities because there is a forest growing between the front door and his children, between the front door and his wife's arms. The forest is made of trees that

bend and cover him. Trees that tell him, "I don't appreciate
ou," and "You should have stayed at work."

These trees grow when the wife thinks of herself first and
doesn't return the love her husband is showing her by his
providing for her. And these trees can cause a husband to
react drastically. You, his wife, have more power than you
realize; power that can be destructive. Sometimes he returns
home to find you "that portion of himself" ready to turn on him
and make him into something quite ugly. Last year there was
an article that appeared in the evening paper: the headline
was: REPORTS HE KILLED CHILDREN FOR WIFE, from
Wilmington, North Carolina, Sept. 8, 197-. A man who said his
wife left him because their children annoyed her led police
yesterday to the bodies of four of his five children. He told
authorities he had killed them in hope that his wife would
return. The fifth child Robert Atlas J   was found in the
same place, seriously injured. All five had been beaten with a
tire tool, authorities said. They ranged in age from 3 to 9 years
old. J   , truck driver, was charged with four counts of
murder and one of assault with a deadly weapon with intent to
kill." Horrible, isn't it? Yes - but it really happened. Dra-
matic - yes. But necessary that we always remember the
truth given to us by God. He made women to fill a need for the
man, and when we do not do that, our man may stop being a
man.

> Yet your desire and craving shall be for your
> husband, and he shall rule over you (Genesis
> 3:16b AV).

Unfortunately many girls get married and believe that
immediately their husband will become a tower of strength.
She wants a man who will become the head of his house
automatically. She hopes that during times of stress he will
instantly supply the strength she needs. But in order to do
this the husband must find his strength somewhere, because
contrary to common thought, man was not born strong. Your
man needs you to be his helpmate, to give him love and understanding, to care for him. And then in return you will find that
"knight in shining armor," the man of the house who will keep
everything standing when it seems ready to crumble. You are
vitally needed to give to him first, so he can return it to you.
Until God showed these things to me our marriage was

miserable. As someone once said, "Jesus envisioned a man as an island. He sailed around man until He found a point of need, and He landed at that point." How many CHRISTIAN women, who profess to follow Christ's example, sail right past their husband's needs, only to be more concerned with their own?

What are a man's points of need? The first one that comes to my mind is his need to be accepted as he is. For some reason when a man and woman get married, the wife has already decided just what he needs to change about himself. Of course SHE doesn't want to be changed, SHE wants to be loved as she is, yet she goes right on trying to change him. I remember specifically thinking that my husband would become a Christian. I also knew that he would eventually stop doing this or that, or start doing something or the other. This must be a particularly bad habit for women. This is evidenced regularly in our classes. It is hard for us to accept our men for exactly what they are, no more and no less.

We all want to be loved for ourselves, not for something we could be. Marriage counselors tell us that more homes are broken by women trying to change their husbands than any other single reason. Yet if you love your husband you must love him as he is. That is true love. Certainly we will all change and grow, but IF YOU DESPERATELY NEED FOR YOUR HUSBAND TO CHANGE BEFORE YOU CAN LOVE HIM, you are being a hypocrite. Instead accept him at face value. He has faults and virtues just as you do. Approach him honestly, realizing that the faults are there but don't be concerned about them. If he wishes to change, that is strictly his business. Love him as God loves us - as we are!

Trying to change a man takes away his freedom, and freedom is the thing a man must have if he would change himself. We cannot talk someone into changing, explain them into changing, or push them into changing. Very often the use of such tactics wil inhibit any changing that might be made if the freedom were there. Stubbornness can draw a veil over any real possibilities and choices for change. And stubbornness is a resistance to force.

Instead relieve his pressures. Let him stop reacting to unhappiness and unfulfilled need. Let him be free to do away

with any bad habits that HE DECIDES HE NEEDS TO BE
RID OF. Many bad habits that we possess are simply
responses to many feelings we have: stinginess, possessive-
ness, jealousy, curtness, etc. You see a man doesn't show his
hurt. He hides his tears and anger is usually displayed in an
attitude rather than in words. You can help him by giving him
sympathy and understanding. We all need these things.

Your husband is no different. He needs someone who will
give him understanding and sympathy but NOT SOMEONE
WHO WILL TRY TO SOLVE HIS PROBLEMS FOR HIM.
His ego is hurt when a woman tries to help him solve his
problems. He needs someone who will tell him he is doing a
good job and who will uplift his spirit. Not someone who will
tell him what he didn't do. He needs a woman who is smart
enough to offer him great assistance without seeming to offer
him any. Don't try to explain his problems to him, show him
his mistakes, or in any other way try to clear his path. He is a
man and has an inner need to face them, to surmount them, if
necessary to stumble over them, but he needs to do it himself.
He needs a woman, whose face is shining with joy, standing on
the side, with faith and admiration beaming from her eyes.

You can accomplish this by several ways. First pray for
wisdom and understanding. It is amazing to see how God can
change lives by giving people insight and knowledge. Then
learn how to give true sympathy. This is done by repeating or
re-expressing what your husband tells you. Then you are
showing you really do understand his problems. For example,
he says, "Boy I really had a tough day at the office today!"
You sympathize by saying, "You must be tired. I'll get you a
glass of iced tea." YOU DON'T SAY, "YOU HAD A TOUGH
DAY TODAY - WHAT DO YOU THINK I HAD, A PICNIC?"
Or another example: he says, "I just don't understand why so
and so has to pick on me!" You say, "I bet it's hard to work
when someone is picking on you." YOU DON'T SAY -
"WELL, DON'T YOU THINK YOU OUGHT TO FIND OUT
WHAT'S BOTHERING HIM?" You don't attempt to find a
solution to his problem and you accept his feelings as being
valid. You express your understanding and sympathy and
affirm your belief that he can handle whatever problem arises,
thereby showing your faith and admiration in his ability as a
man.

A man needs your admiration, your comfort, your love, but he can't tell you about his needs. He cannot say how much you mean to him because that would be admitting his needs and he feels that would be weakness. He will often find it hard to tell you how much he loves you because that is the way he is. He will not talk a lot about his feelings and thoughts because that is the way he is. A man is different. He shows his anger only in times of great stress and wears gentleness most of the time. But behind that gentleness rests the anger and fire that takes men to war protecting their family and home. Behind that gentle quietness rests the determination that makes kings war against kings. Accept him as he is and love him in spite of the fact that you can't get him to express himself as you would want him to do.

IF YOUR HUSBAND ISN'T A CHRISTIAN

I want to stop here and speak specifically to women whose husbands aren't Christians. All of the information in this book can be specifically applied to you, to your life, and to your husband. Everything can be useful toward helping him desire to have Christ in his life. But there are more thoughts for you to directly tackle.

For one thing, we are what we feel. We behave according to what we believe. In other words, your husband's actions are determined by what he feels and believes. He may not say what he believes, but he will act according to his beliefs. Belief is our basic conviction about important aspects of living. A man may not consciously know what he believes but his actions will tell on him. For example, if a man believes the world is basically made of people who will try to cheat him, he will constantly try to protect himself from people. If he believes that the people he works with aren't worthwhile, he will not establish any kind of friendly relationship with them. There are many subtle ways you can discover just how your husband feels about things, strictly by observing his actions. This certainly applies to his beliefs about Christians and about the church.

I hope you can be aware of how your husband believes, simply so you can pray specifically about him. Also I feel that if you understand him by observing him, you can have more patience. You know, God is so great and can accomplish such marvelous things when we turn them over to him. I remember realizing that my husband simply drives too fast. I worried a lot about his traveling on the job. And of course while I was worrying, I was inhibiting God's power by my lack of faith. So when I finally realized that and prayed about it, some changes took place. Bill just happened to pass the scene of a terrible accident that made an impression which lasted for a long time. I know his driving speed dropped at least 10 m.p.h. And later he went to work for Volkswagen and I told him that I really felt like God had answered another prayer by placing him in a company car that had a smoother ride at lower speeds and definitely was not designed for really fast driving.

Another important evaluation for you to make is whether your husband has gained a measure of maturity. Maturity is acquired by experience, growth in years, understanding, and upbringing. If a child is raised to be responsible and understanding, he will probably have maturity 50% in hand. The rest will come naturally as life's experiences deal it out. We all have immaturities that we expect others to suffer through with us and men are no strangers to it either. So understand this and have patience as you pray that God will direct your lives and guide you both through the immaturities that you have. I believe it takes a more mature person to realize his need for God.

Lack of perfection also holds many men back from Christ. Your husband may feel that he can never be good enough to be a Christian. This is a real stumbling block to many people. Christ died to save SINNERS. God loved SINNERS (John 3:16) so much that he gave His son for us. But sometimes we get to feeling pretty comfortable about ourselves, and think that after all, we attend church, we help other people, we try to live a Christian life, etc. But stop and think about this - how often do we treat other people as if that were true? Do you treat your husband as if he should be perfect? Do you tell him he shouldn't do this or that? Isn't that judging standards of perfection?

Instead let a man see Christ in you. When someone turns to Christ they will automatically begin to let go of other things. So let him be. God loves him with all of his weakness and sinful ways - just as he loves you with all of your weakness and sinful ways. This was brought to my attention strongly when our family began reading through a children's book of Bible stories. These stories began with Adam and Eve, touched all the well-known stories through the Old and New Testaments. And as we finished the last story I was struck by the fact that so many of the characters in the stories were sinful. They lied, cheated, killed, didn't obey God, lived in adultery, and had no faith. Yet God forgave their sins. He forgave them their past. He was merciful and loving to them. He didn't hold it over their heads the rest of their lives - he forgave and forgot.

So it is extremely important that you show this forgiveness to your non-Christian husband (or anyone else). Forgive your husband. He who cannot forgive others, breaks the bridge over which he himself must pass if he is to reach heaven. Everyone has the need to be forgiven. And your husband or any other non-Christian has the need to see forgiveness in you before he can see it in the Father. And it would also follow that you would admit your own imperfections to others. Naturally we all want to strive toward a perfection we can see in the distance and we will advance further with God's help in our lives. So when we let people know that God is helping us we will be giving them even more understanding about how great it is to be a Christian.

We want to make Christ come alive for others by showing them patience and love. Realize that our background is responsible for most of the feelings we have about Christ. For example, suppose that you were raised in a family that practiced no religion at all? You had no knowledge of God. You would feel, "Who is God, and what can He do for me?" You would say, "I'm doing just fine as I am." Other people who were raised with teaching about God will naturally feel quite differently. Perhaps you were raised by a family that taught you the wrong things about God. Maybe you grew up feeling that God hates all bad people and that God only listens to people who follow his law perfectly. Could you be interested in talking to a God like this? Even though we are all basically lonely people and want someone to listen to and understand us, even though no one really can understand us completely except God, can't you see that you wouldn't understand this because of your background? Neither can your husband understand many things simply because of who he is. So accept that and patiently love him, treat him kindly, even though you don't agree with his beliefs.

There is always the chance that your husband will become interested in Christianity. Certainly because of your Christ-like example, but also because religious tendencies occur in all human beings. This hunger shows up in all people sometime. It reoccurs at times of stress, nostalgia and urgent need. It builds to a peak during adolescence and reoccurs at times of crisis.

> He has made everything beautiful in its time;
> He also has planted eternity in men's heart
> and mind (a divinely implanted sense of a
> purpose working through the ages which
> nothing under the sun, but only God, can
> satisfy), yet so that man cannot find out what
> God has done from the beginning to the end
> (Ecclesiastes 3:11 AV).

So whether he will admit it or not, whether he knows it or not, he has an inner need for God. Different barriers are set up by different people - depending upon their own needs, under-standings, upbringing, and maturity—but THE NEED IS THERE.

So take the steps that I have outlined in this chapter seriously. Fulfill your husband's needs by being a good Christian helpmate while always letting him know what Christ means to YOU. Pray constantly with a definite request when you see by his actions what he believes and therefore what he needs help with. And finally make a new beginning with your husband if you have a past record of not being the kind of wife he needs, by telling him that you have realized your lack - and that you know how important he is to you. Let him know that you have faith in him. Look for his good points and tell him how much you appreciate him. Then expect that if not before, certainly during a time of crisis or emotional frustration he may decide he wants to know more about Christ, so be ready to explain to him in simple terms exactly what Christ means to you.

Whether your husband is a Christian or not, you will want to have a good relationship with him. I have found in my life that all of the above points in this chapter are, without exception, very important toward this end. A good marriage is one of the greatest blessings that God has given us. And if you follow God's will toward loving your husband you will find that he feels you are the greatest blessing he could receive. Then he will say:

I AM BLESSED

In an age
When it's fashionable
to be cool, and smart -
Not to make commitments
But to seek many companions
I found someone
Who gallantly
Pledged to love one person
And no other
As long as we both
Should live.

In an age
When it's considered
The in thing
To travel light - keep movin',
And work people
To get to the top,
I found someone
With simple tastes
Who merely wanted
To serve others,
To be part of a family -
To care for children.

In this age
Of fragile friendships
Blown minds,
Freaked out fellows -
THANK GOD, I FOUND A CHRISTIAN

(From I AM BLESSED, by Mary Ann Malone: **Christian Woman Magazine**; R. B. Sweet, Publisher)

A HUSBAND

The Man in Charge

You have put him in charge of everything you made; everything is put under his authority: all sheep and oxen, and wild animals too, the birds and fish, and all the life in the sea (Psalms 8:6 LB).

A Partner

You husbands must be careful of your wives, being thoughtful of their needs and honoring them as the weaker sex. Remember that you and your wife are partners in receiving God's blessings, and if you don't treat her as you should, your prayers will not get ready answers (1 Peter 3:7 LB).

Love Wife

And you husbands, show the same kind of love to your wives as Christ showed to the church when he died for her, to make her holy and clean, washed by baptism and God's Word; so that he could give her to himself as a glorious church without a single spot or wrinkle or any other blemish, being holy and without a single fault. That is how husbands should treat their wives, loving them as parts of themselves. For since a man and his wife are now one, a man is really doing himself a favor and loving himself when he loves his wife! (Ephesians 5:25-28 LB).

Love Him

If I gave everything I have to poor people, and if I were burned alive for preaching the Gospel but didn't love others, it would be of no value whatever (1 Corinthians 13:3 LB).

Don't Love Money

Stay away from the love of money; be satisfied with what you have. For God has said, "I will never, never fail you nor forsake you" (Hebrews 13:5 LB).

Have Good Deeds

Just as the body is dead when there is no spirit in it, so faith is dead if it is not the kind that results in good deeds (James 2:26 LB).

Put God First

If you want favor with both God and man, and a reputation for good judgment and common sense, then trust the Lord completely; don't ever trust yourself. In everything you do, put God first, and He will direct you and crown your efforts with success (Proverbs 3:4-6 LB).

arriage

Chapter 9

> This is a profound mystery - but I am talking
> about Christ and the church. However, each
> one of you also must love his wife as he loves
> himself, and the wife must respect her
> husband (Ephesians 5:32,33 NIV).

> ...for we are members of his body. For this
> reason a man will leave his father and mother
> and will be united to his wife, and the two will
> become one flesh (Ephesians 5:30,31 NIV).

The Bible tells us that God made man and woman in a
specific way for a special purpose. The first man and woman
were created to live together.

> "This is it!" Adam exclaimed. "She is part of
> my own bone and flesh! Her name is 'woman'
> because she was taken out of a man" (Genesis
> 2:23 LB).

And marriage brings the man and woman, who were
separated, back together again.

> For although the first woman came out of man,
> all men have been born from women ever
> since, and both men and women come from
> God their Creator (1 Corinthians 11:12 LB).

This union is both spiritual and physical. The sexual desire
that we experience is not just part of our physical need, it is
part of our deep spiritual need to put back together what God
purposed. This is part of our inner nature to return a man and
a woman into one being. I like the way William Banowsky
explains this:

In other words, man was created not simply as a separate individual but as a mysterious sexual duality of which male and female are the components, the relational poles. This sexual differentiation is not, as with the lower species, simply for the purpose of procreation. No mere biological appendage for populating the earth or for bringing pleasure. This sexual distinction exists essentially in the NATURE OF MAN. We are saying that manhood means more than maleness or femaleness, which after all, would simply be sex in isolation. The significance of manhood and womanhood resides, not in what each is unto itself, but IN WHAT EACH HAS BEEN MADE TO BECOME TO THE OTHER. Each yearns to know mutual completeness which is possible only in communion with the other. Marriage is God's miracle of restoring the two into one. Two people - perfectly complementary yet as radically different as they can be - man and woman - innately hunger to immerse their separate prior selves into ONE COMPLETE SELF. (From THE NEW MORALITY: A CHRISTIAN SOLUTION, By William Banowsky; R. B. Sweet, Publishers)

"Long before the coming of Sigmund Freud, the author of Genesis understood this very clearly and spelled out the profound relationship between sex and human nature. The book's fifth chapter opens with a little read creation account shedding much light on human sexuality. 'God created man, in the likeness of God made he him; male and female created he them, and blessed THEM and called THEIR NAME ADAM, in the day when they were created (Genesis 5:2).' " Mr. Banowsky goes on to explain, "Those who have neglected this passage in favor of the earlier creation accounts will be surprised to see that, at the very beginning, Adam was not the name of the man and Eve of the woman, but that the word 'Adam' - the Hebrew term meaning mankind - designated both the first man and the first woman.

Isn't that a beautiful description of the marriage of a man and a woman. Many times we think we are drawn to one another first because of a physical attraction that is strong. And that is true, but it is true because of our spiritual nature. And a marriage can remain successful and happy after the two individuals have been joined, if both partners love each other as God has described - a love that also is referred to as the love that Christ has for the church.

On the part of the man, he loves the wife as he loves himself. He protects her, takes care of her, and comforts her. On the part of the woman, she seeks constantly to please him and finds her highest happiness in doing what her husband wants her to do. Both man and wife caring just as Christ and the church care for each other.

Of course, this is the ideal situation, and you are probably thinking, "That's really great, but how do we accomplish this?" There are certainly more unsuccessful marriages around for us to observe - possibly our own. Bill and I had an unsuccessful marriage at one point. And I feel that everything in this chapter had some bearing on our marriage becoming better. Thankfully, we were forced into the realization that we needed to make some changes. There are many couples who are on very shaky ground but they have not come to the point of separation or divorce yet.

Some couples remain married and wish they weren't. The prospect of divorce has occurred to them at one time or another but for some reason it was shoved aside. For others the thought has not occurred to them yet, but when a time of stress occurs they will find they have no resources to pull them through.

Do you have the kind of love that Christ and the church have for each other? Do problems tend to separate you further? Do you depend only on yourself instead of allowing your husband to assume his responsibilities? Do you both function as separate individuals? Does your husband love you with the kind of love Christ has for the church - a protecting, cherishing love?

Do you pay attention to what your husband wants you to do? I feel that a woman who has no concern for what her husband wants is selfish. I had been very selfish in our marriage. And it is an easy rut for any woman to fall into. If you want to spend your husband's money the way YOU want then you are as I was - thoughtless and domineering. When a woman wants to love her husband only on her own terms, she is thoughtless and unloving. She is a hypocrite and she certainly doesn't love him as the church loves Christ.

The tie that binds a husband and a wife together in a successful marriage is tender, thoughtful, utterly selfless and constantly protective. Regardless of how you feel your husband is making his half of the marriage work, ARE YOU MAKING YOUR HALF WORK IN THE PROPER WAY?

When a marriage isn't working out, we always believe it is the other person's fault. Perhaps you feel that your husband mistreats you and you shouldn't have to take that kind of treatment. You have found out through the years that your husband is obstinate, stubborn, ridiculous and unloving. He absolutely will not change about anything. You see your marriage as one that cannot be changed; there is no use trying any longer.

I know there are rare cases where this is true. One apparent example of this can be found in 1 Samuel 25:3-42 where the story of Abigail unfolds. Abigail was a woman who had beauty, wisdom and courage. She also had faith in God and had made a commitment to follow God's will - completely. She had an unsuccessful marriage by today's standards. Her husband was a foolish man and she missed out on all the things that we count as important in marriage. He was undoubtedly cruel. Yet she stayed a loving and tactful wife. She even kept David from killing him though her own life would have been better if he were dead. Later then he did die through God's judgment and Abigail was given a better life than the one she had had.

But normally, when a marriage is weak or failing marriage counselors and social workers will tell us that both parties are wrong. Then we get into that old question; which came first the chicken or the egg, the husband's wrong or the wife's wrong. And there is never an answer to that.

Divorce is not the answer. The divorce rate rises each year as more and more marriages break up. It has become easier to obtain a divorce, and because there is less stigma attached to divorce by the general public, and because we hear about unhappy people released from bad circumstances, we too can begin to look at divorce as a possible answer. But listen to what one lady said after she had gotten a divorce:

> I obtained my divorce believing that it would be a release from certain fears and worries I had. I knew I would have to earn a livelihood. That was alright. But what I didn't know was the emotional cost I would have to pay. It took years to recover from the death of my marriage and no one can ever understand or sympathize unless they have gone through it. Divorce is never a clean cut operation; the scars remain and the persons who are involved end up feeling like an extra finger. The children suffer. They need so much from you and you need so much yourself. You find you can't give them everything THEY need because YOU are so emotionally drained yourself. Even though their father may be the worst, you believe, he remains a male figure to them and could have given them a feeling of family protection. He could have given them an attitude toward you as being part of that family, not as being the TOTAL FAMILY. It is worth trying every means possible to save a marriage if only to save the children the hurt when they enter school and have to admit they only have one parent. Other problems can't be seen in advance, such as how your time is filled with working, mothering and keeping house, so there is no time or energy left over for dating or entertaining. When you do go out the children have to be left with someone or taken along and neither feels very comfortable. You'll also know that you'll probably make the same mistakes the second time should you try to remarry. Statistics bear this out and you begin to wonder what is the matter with you. In order to spare yourself and the children this agony, go as far as you can to make a marriage work, then go even farther. Life always has problems even when

it is at its best. Don't envy married friends
who seem to be having happiness. THEY
MAY BE WORKING AT IT HARDER THAN
YOU. Think before you drop one load of
problems and pick up a different set.
(Excerpts from "A Divorcee Speaks", an-
onymously written for the 20TH CENTURY
CHRISTIAN, Nashville, Tennessee.)

But fixing a marriage is hard; sometimes it seems
impossible. Yet trying to keep a bad marriage together
without fixing it seems also impossible. Why waste years that
could be joyous and happy, years that could be filled with
love?

Many people try to fix up their marriages by going to a
marriage counselor, or by reading marriage books, or by
talking to friends, yet still find failure. But success is possible.
When our second daughter was on the way, Bill and I decided
that we had to do something or we would either end up with a
bad marriage or a divorce. It wasn't easy and it wasn't any
fun - but it was better than all the alternatives. Looking back
now, we can laugh about a lot of things that weren't laughable
then. We were miserable! It's easy to forget painful things in
retrospect. Before it had been like being in a prison - and now
it's like being in the sunlight. And when you are in the light
you just aren't inclined to look back into the darkness much.
Besides, there were many happy times that occurred even
when we were having problems. Looking back we know that
the struggle was definitely worthwhile. We have agreed that
we would both go back and do it all over again, because,
painful or not, the results are special. Many people go on year
after year and never make the effort that is necessary to have
a successful marriage. We're glad we did.

Persistence was one of the important reasons we made it.
My grandfather used to say - KEEP ON, KEEPING ON. Success does not come from giving up. We will each have special
problems that are really difficult to solve, but with
determination and faith changes will occur. We went to a
marriage counselor and through him we were able to see each
other's needs. Counseling can really help, but only if the
couple's goals are set toward succeeding. We knew that we
wanted the ultimates of all the good things that make up a

marriage. Each marriage is unique, but each marriage can have a joining in spirit, in love, in body, and in understanding. Through prayer we found the ability to see what we should do.

God does the very best repair job. Marriages will automatically be strengthened by understanding God's will and then by following it. If, for éxample, you were learning to drive, you would first state your desire that you wanted to learn, then you would begin the lessons. Now your learning how to drive comes from someone else's previous knowledge. You have never driven before so you don't know which pedal makes the car move and which pedal makes the car stop. But you certainly do not try to go against what the teacher tells you by trying to step on the brake to make the car move. Instead you listen and pay attention. Then you do as you are taught.

The same principle is involved in following God's advice. God made us. He made us to work best a certain way. We have no previous knowledge about what makes a successful marriage. So each day we try to find out more and more about what God's will is for a successful marriage.

God's will for Christian women is that she follow the outlines given about women in the Bible. She is to be a wife to her husband and a mother to her children by functioning under her husband's authority. She should not usurp authority. She is to be a helper. She is to adapt herself to her husband. These commandments are given because of our basic natures.

A marriage that is happy revolves around a true realization of the differences between a husband and a wife. Then a wife can bring to marriage her deep feelings (sensitivity), warmth, compassion, submission, kindness, love, and the managing of the household. The husband brings to marriage the assumption of the leadership role, decision making, providing financial means, and setting the moral and spiritual values. He is the head. She is the heart. Together they have a partnership which allows them to reach goals together that never could be obtained without the successful partnership.

I had not followed that guideline in our marriage. I was too much of a helper. Now everytime I read that word "Helper" I have to laugh. Because for quite a few years I was such a helper that I nearly destroyed our marriage. I helped by telling my husband what to do, what not to do, and how to do. I felt that I was helping him, keeping him from making mistakes. And somehow even though we loved each other very much, our relationship began to change. Bill was no longer the kind, considerate boy I had married. He made decisions that made no sense - I told him about them, helping him to understand why they were bad. I didn't realize that I was directly disobeying God's will that a wife should be as the church is to Christ.

I was not loving my husband by my actions. As the church loves Christ by its actions, so a wife should constantly be loving her husband as if she were showing love to Christ. A wife should trust her husband's judgments even if she does not understand or agree with them. She should learn to be quiet. Her mouth should not come between them. It is alright to have an opinion and to express it freely, but after you have expressed it, you and your husband should both know that you will COMPLETELY allow him to do it his way WITHOUT ANY REPERCUSSIONS if he chooses to differ from you. And if his judgment turns out to be bad, your reply should be, "Everyone makes mistakes dear, so don't feel bad about it." Or, "You did what you thought was best and I'm proud of your decision even if it didn't turn out as you had hoped."

Give your husband your complete confidence. Give it to him freely, realizing that if you were a man, you couldn't take on any job and do it well - unless you had the confidence of the people around you. And while you are giving him your backing, turn everything over to God. Put your deep confidence in God to make everything turn out alright.

Many women cannot give their husband the rule of their home because of their own fears and anxieties. They are afraid he won't take care of things. They don't trust his judgment and ability. He has made mistakes so he will naturally make more - he may even make the same mistakes again. And knowing how the wife feels, the man DOES NOT DO THE JOB WELL. Then we aren't following God's will.

It was thus that Sarah obeyed Abraham (following his guidance and acknowledging his headship over her by) calling him Lord-master, leader, authority. And now you are her true daughters if you do right and let nothing terrify you - not giving way to hysterical fears or letting anxieties unnerve you (1 Peter 3:6 AV).

So we are to call our husband our Lord, master, leader, authority, meanwhile not giving way to our fears or anxieties. And then we will be freeing him to begin acting in a responsible way. Many times a man acts badly simply because he is frustrated at his own inability to cope with a woman who is not following God's will for a wife. Sometimes a man will mistreat a woman either verbally, physically, or mentally, simply because he knows no other way to react to his own frustrations. These frustrations arise because he isn't being treated as the man of his house, the man that God made him to be.

The immediate question that often follows this is, "But what about him treating me as the wife God made me to be?" Naturally this is an important question too. But because I am a woman, I don't feel that I should speak to men about this question. If you have this problem in your life, your husband isn't loving you as God tells him to - there is one answer I can give you. I know that in most cases even though the husband is doing things wrong and may not be accepting his part of the marriage responsibilities, YOU, A CHRISTIAN WOMAN have the POWER to make your marriage whole. I've seen it happen in the lives of many couples.

With God's help a Christian can make a difference in a marriage. First - by following God's will as we've studied in previous paragraphs, but most of all by becoming a loving, kind, patient, concerned and trusting wife. God will help you understand your husband's actions. This will give you the ability to have patience. God will show you your husband's strong points - so you can look at them instead of looking at his faults. God will help you be a loving and kind wife by showing you that you don't need to hope your husband will change, but rather need to accept him as he is right now. There always remains the chance that your husband will change in response to you. This is the hope that you need to have only if you really accept your husband as he is and LOVE HIM.

Love is the most important ingredient!

THE GREATEST OF THESE

Reason faces up to life
And sees things as they are
Hope sees things as they ought to be,
And wishes on a star.
Faith dreams of miracles to come
That only God can do;
Love goes to work with patient hands
To make these dreams come true.
(Aim for a Star, by Helen Lowrie Marshall,
Doubleday & Co., Publishers)

Marriage is not just the wedding dress, guests, and a honeymoon. A marriage is a promise before God that is to last as long as you both shall live. Honor that promise with everything you have. Bind that promise together with love as you both face the periods of straining and testing which will occur. Remember -

Love is caring
Love is being patient when you don't feel patient
Love is being kind when you feel unkind
Love is being happy when you see something that is good
    for someone else, even if it isn't good for YOU.
Love is bearing up under anything and everything that
    comes - always ready to believe the best of your husband.
Love has a non-fading hope, no matter the circumstances.
Love says "I'm sorry," even when you did no wrong.
Love never fails.

You can endure everything without weakening when you love
    someone.
You will never envy other's good fortune, when you love them.
You will never be jealous of another's happiness, when you
    love them.
You will never be boastful or spiteful or bitter, just to get
    even, when you love him.
You will never tear him down, just to get even, when you love
    him.

You will never tell him you could have done it better, when you love him.

You will never tell him something "for his own good" when you love him.

You will never be too proud to say you were wrong, when you love him.

You will never insist he do things your way, even if you are right, if you love him.

You won't be touchy, fretful, or resentful, if you love him.

You won't even remember the bad things he has done, if you love him.

YOU WILL BE AS MUCH LIKE GOD AS YOU CAN - WHEN YOU LOVE HIM.

How can you attain this kind of love? Begin by looking at problems from his point of view. You will gain "empathy" for your husband by stepping into his shoes, trying to understand how he feels. (Stop thinking about how you feel also.) You know, God loves us even when there is a problem separating us from Him. Perhaps this is because God knows why we are the way we are. He knows why we are weak, and he knows why we fail. He may not like our imperfections or the way we give in and react to outside pressures but He does understand and He does love us still. I know you will find that you can love your husband in a way that is more like God's love for us, if you will continually strive to put yourself in his shoes.

POINT OF VIEW

A weighty problem might be
Likened to a mountain tall,
With you and I sincere
In our belief we see it all,
When actually, we only see,
The side within our view,
Small wonder you're at odds with me
And I at odds with you.

But if I made an effort
To cross over to your side

And if you too, sincerely try
To scale the Great Divide
We're bound to find there at the peak
A common meeting place
Where we can see each other's side
As we meet, face to face.

And problems, just like mountains
Can be conquered if we do
Our best to reach the point
Where we can see the other's view.

When you honestly try to see your husband's point of view (whether or not you agree with it is beside the point entirely), communication will begin to improve. Especially if you let him know that you see his point of view. When a conversation comes up about a problem and he explains his point of view, you can simply let him know that you have heard what he has said. Tell him, "I see what you mean, honey." You aren't saying that you agree or disagree but rather that you see that he is trying to work out an answer and that you respect his right and ability to do that.

You will then be initiating pleasant and uplifting conversation. Communication is an important key to having a healthy marriage.

Kind words are like honey - enjoyable and healthful (Proverbs 16:24 LB).

But we need to learn what makes up good communication. We all know that ALL communication can't be pleasant and sweet, but we do know that arguing only provokes arguing. So in between these two extremes rests the communication we are looking for.

Good communication is smooth, enjoyable, and free from fear. It will keep everything else running perfectly. It begins with a removal of fear.

When one person speaks to another person, the reaction of the listener is important. When your husband tells you something that upsets you, and you react by getting upset, you are forcing him to make a choice the next time he wants to be honest with you. Men are the strongest creatures on earth except when it comes to facing a woman and taking the chance of upsetting her. So next time he will either (1) not tell you at all, or (2) he will lie or cover over the story in some way. You, the listener, have kept the communicator from telling the truth.

Now I know at this point you are probably feeling that YOU have to do everything and your husband doesn't have to do anything. And of course you may be right, depending on whether your husband wants a successful marriage or not. But what you need to see is that when he tells you about something that has happened or will happen, he is making an effort to build a successful marriage. He is making an effort to communicate. You, the listener, have the power to allow him to continue talking or to turn him off.

When you are the communicator, you do the same thing. But this is probably such a subtle decision on your part that you hardly realize you are making one. (Neither does your husband totally realize his decisions on communication.) You may have a relative or a friend that you are sensitive about talking with them because everytime you say something, they take it differently than you had hoped they would. So you find yourself either avoiding them or talking to them about inconsequential things. This way you miss the embarrassment of their reaction. It's the same for your husband. Because of fear of your reaction he makes the same decisions. Another good example of this can be seen in children. Children lie because they are afraid of telling the truth, afraid that they will be punished and afraid of ruining their parent's good thoughts about them. And grownups are no different. Occasionally someone will be honest in all of their conversations with others no matter what reactions they will receive. But this is BECAUSE THEY HAVE DEVELOPED AN INSENSITIV-ITY TO REACTIONS. They don't really care how anyone else feels about their thinking. BUT A HUSBAND DOES CARE. He cares desperately. You are his other half, part of him, and who of us would wish that when the words come out of our mouth, our hand would then come up and slap our face. That's what happens in many conversations between husband and wife. Yet God has clearly told us that the husband is in charge (that means we don't make the decisions, so if he wants to do something differently we aren't given the right to expect him to do it our way). We have been told to "adapt." And I certainly expect my hand to adapt to what my head has decided to do, otherwise we would have a ridiculous situation. I could do absolutely nothing. It is the same in marriage.

The only way a wife can change and help her husband get over this, is by years of listening to him, and loving him, and accepting him, until eventually he will not fear her reaction but will know that she loves and admires him. Listening has some finer points. A good listener does not judge. The person talking will have no fear of recriminations or loss of faith on the part of the one listening. Let your husband know that you have heard what he has said. Let him know that you appreciate hearing his thinking on the matter. Really appreciate and admire him.

Then when you have something you would like to talk about - some problem that needs to be aired or a question you need an answer for - be the talker that understands what communication is all about. Many times when a man and a woman begin to talk, the man feels at a complete disadvantage because his wife brings out all of the old skeletons in the closet, all of the past mistakes he has made, and all of the problems they have been through. SHE HAS NOT FORGIVEN OR FORGOTTEN ANY OF THEM. So be loving as you discuss what is on your mind. State the problem as you see it. Then listen to what he has to say. Really listen. Put yourself into his shoes again and try to figure out how he sees the problem. Listen for his solution. If you feel that his solution isn't quite acceptable then you should be able to state your reasons for this feeling. State them honestly and clearly but don't intentionally say anything that will hurt your husband. Don't try to force your opinion on him either. And if after hearing your reasons why you feel his solution would not be as good, he still asserts his solution, then you should accept it as being the one that God wills. Above all, never let your acceptance of his solution include a bad attitude, non-agreement expressed in any way or a feeling that all will fail. Trust him by trusting God to work everything out.

Let your husband know that you trust him. Let him know you see his potential also. We all like for others to see what we hope we are. God sees the potential in each of us and looking back over our lives and the way that God has guided us, we can realize a new and different goal than any we would have set for ourselves. Your husband can do the same thing if he sees your love and admiration through the years. You can show it to him by letting him know you see his potential.

CAUSE AND EFFECT

Once, someone said something nice about me.
And all undeserved though I knew it to be,
I treasured it there on my heart's deepest shelf,
Til one day I quite surprised even myself
By honestly making an effort to be
That nice thing that somebody said about me!
(From Dare to Be Happy, by Helen Lowrie Marshall, Doubleday and Co., publisher)

The man who likes to play with little children has some understanding of a child's feelings. He may not realize this but you can see it and point it out. A husband who realizes that his wife isn't feeling well and leaves her alone might be displaying some understanding of a woman. A wise wife can also point this out. Look for all of the things that your husband tells you by his actions, and then point them out to him. He will love you for seeing his best points.

Learning not to argue is a useful step into better communication. Refuse to argue. If your husband comes in and is tired, listen to what he has to say and if you disagree simply keep it to yourself. If he insists on arguing about something, learn how to apologize whether or not you feel you have done something wrong. Let him know you are sorry that he is upset. Sacrifice yourself to his needs and God will see that you are given back everything you have sacrificed and more.

Compromise is also important in communication. Problems that seem to have no answer can be compromised. This is a way you can say, "I love you. Even though your solution seems unacceptable to me, I will give in on part of it."

This can help in the cases where an answer seems strictly impossible any other way.

Don't abuse your use of communication. Remember that:

He who has knowledge spares his words, and a man of understanding has a cool spirit (Proverbs 17:27 AV).

Even a fool when he holds his peace is considered wise; when he closes his lips he is esteemed a man of understanding (Proverbs 17:28 AV).

It is better to dwell in a desert land than with a contentious woman and vexation (Proverbs 21:19 AV).

Better is a dry morsel with quietness than a house full of feasting with strife (Proverbs 17:1 AV).

A continual dripping on a day of violent showers and a contentious woman are alike (Proverbs 27:15 AV).

He who covers and forgives an offense seeks love, but he who repeats or harps on a matter separates even close friends (Proverbs 17:9 AV).

Good communication and all that it embodies can help establish important areas of responsibility that surround a marriage. This was an important point that we learned at the marriage counselors. The husband has his job and the wife shouldn't try to help him run it. The wife also has her job and the husbasnd shouldn't tell her how to run it. Communication can help establish the different areas of work in each individual marriage.

Use your communication to assure human dignity and fairness for yourself as the wife. Observe all the rules, though, don't punch, jab, or slice at your husband when you talk to him. Tell him with love that as a woman WHO WANTS TO MAKE HIM HAPPY, you need to have him verbalize his love now and then; you need to share his life at work a little and want him to tell you about it; you need for him to set the guidelines in disciplining the children; you need to have some time for yourself so you can rejuvinate and therefore be more loving to him and to the children. After you have spoken about what you need, if your husband doesn't immediately pick up on it, then let it drop completely. Don't continue mentioning it over and over. Accept the fact that it isn't God's will for there to be a change in that area of need yet. Place it completely in God's hands and know that when it is time for something to happen in that area, it will. God can handle it.

God can take care of your children. It is important that you accept this and trust God, because children can come between two people in a marriage. They can create serious problems simply because the wife doesn't follow God's teaching on this either. And when children find out that the parents are disagreeing about something they will push even more. They will try everything they can because children are naturally selfish and they want to be allowed to do what they want to do. But when the wife adapts to her husband's authority in this, the children will find no crack to make into a crevice. Even if you disagree with your husband's methods, it is vitally important that you give in to him so that you can both handle the children consistently. Educators agree that discipline is only good when it is given to the children in a consistent manner. If you disagree with your husband strongly, then save it until you are alone and the children will not even be aware that there is a disagreement. And remember - speak not in anger about how you feel, but with the hope that you can understand why he feels the way he does, because God has given him the authority to decide.

And if you cannot abide his decision - then accept it anyway and turn it all over to God. God can handle even that. You will have to be patient and know that there are things in your husband's life that cause him to act the way he does. Sometimes it takes awhile for God to work through some of these things. In the meantime, trust God, that your children will not suffer from being either over-disciplined or under-disciplined, but only by being inconsistently disciplined.

After the problems that children cause in marriage, money follows a close second. More arguments occur because of money and the lack of it, than for any other reason. But the Bible tells us not to be a lover of money. And many of the arguments that occur are because there is not enough money for some luxury. Again, the husband and the wife usually disagree about what is a luxury and what isn't. My husband, for example, feels that having someone paint the house is a necessity. I think it is a luxury. But in order to be the kind of wife that God wants me to be, I have only mentioned it once when the original decision was made to have the house painted. And I have mentioned afterwards how nice it was to have someone come in and paint the house, because I want him to know that I respect his decision and have even found joy in it. You should do the same thing when your husband decides between a luxury or a necessity.

I believe that most of the money problems that occur come about because the wife handles the money. Now we started out with Bill handling the money. After a few years I took over. Then he did it again for awhile. Then I did it for awhile. Nothing was ever satisfactory because even when I was handling the money, he was making the decisions about what was to be spent. And then when things became hard for me to handle I would give it all back to him to do. Usually it was handed over with great disgust on my part. Then he would take charge while I questioned everything he was doing. This was still unsatisfactory. I believe that now we know why neither way worked.

God put man in charge. He needs to learn how to handle the money. And he won't learn how unless he has the practical experience of doing it and making mistakes. Now those mistakes may be hard for both the husband and the wife to get over, but they are necessary and important to the learning process. Mothers go through the same process as they raise the children. We make many mistakes. Some of them very costly to our children's mental or physical being. But that is life and unless the wife realizes that, she will never be a kind and understanding wife as her husband learns about finances as he alternately sinks and swims. Then when he decides what is a luxury, he will really know - because he has gone through a difficult schooling. But allow him to do what God felt that man could handle. Otherwise you aren't having faith in God. And God can handle it.

God can provide you with the help you need financially. One of the ladies in class just told me the other day how God answered her recent prayer for help. She works on a monthly project for Christian women which requires buying some materials. She couldn't get any money from her husband so she turned it over to God. Soon after she was asked if she would babysit with a darling little girl that not only fit into her family perfectly, but also answered a deep inner cry. The lady wanted to have more children but her husband refuses to, so now she has a baby to love too. Isn't God marvelous?

Another important problem to many marriages are the relatives. The Bible clearly states that when a couple are married they become as one and leave mother and father. But you have probably seen how many still belong to mom and dad. They have borrowed money and now they not only owe them the money, but they owe them more time, and they owe them their life. They will never be able to pay what they owe because their indebtedness goes much beyond just money. Now how can two people learn how to live as one with mutual inter-dependance when there are other people involved? It is no wonder that the Scriptures state this so clearly. "A man leaves his father and mother." It is against not only God's law but also against common sense to try to build a marriage when any outside forces are pulling at that marriage. Your only indebtedness to your parents is love. Nothing more. So whatever you feel expresses your love to your parents that is what you should do. But don't try to pay back the fact that they had you.

Your parents should not expect you to pay back the debt of being born. I don't believe that parents should help their children financially, either. Because if they do the children will never learn responsibility as quickly. If you have no experience handling money, how will you ever learn. And if you have never had to be responsible for your own debts, how will you ever learn what your debt limit is? So don't let your parents spoil you, hobble you, with help. They will not only deter the normal learning process but in return they will feel that they owe you their opinions, their judgments, their beliefs, and their interference. Parents only owe their children love.

A Christian woman owes her husband some things also. She would be trustworthy. She would have control over herself so that her husband would know he could trust her with the car, the charge-plate, the children, their home, and last but not least - her own body.

> A worthy wife is her husband's joy and crown;
> the other kind corrodes his strength and tears
> down everything he does (Proverbs 12:4 LB).

Your attitude would reflect Christ. You would treat every day as if it were a gift from God. And you wouldn't expect everything to come up roses all of the time. You would understand that God is in charge of everything. And you would pass that on to your husband by the soft and gentle way you speak and act. You can do that because you know that God is working in the lives of your family and that problems make us all grow and change. So you would accept problems with peace in your heart. You wouldn't pick on your husband's sins but would spend that time looking at your own self. You would ask yourself if you had been cold, sarcastic, a spendthrift, harsh, or lazy. By the time you finished your own self evaluation you would completely forget about anything you would like to criticize about your husband.

A Christian woman will above all not let incompatability enter her marriage. INCOME can be a problem in any marriage but it won't be such a problem if the wife is COMPATABLE. A Christian woman will be eager and happy to be available to her husband - no headaches, no excuses, but gladness that God has allowed her to be a partaker in one of the richest blessings of marriage. (God has said that a woman doesn't have charge over her own body. But too often we skip over this teaching) So don't withhold your body as punishment because your husband has done something you don't like. Instead prepare yourself mentally and physically to love your husband as God loves you. TOTALLY.

When you have accomplished the task of becoming the wife God wants you to be, with His help, you will also find that you are the beneficiary of some of the most glorious words a woman can hear.

> There are many fine women in the world but you are the best of them all (Proverbs 31:29 LB).

A good marriage brings many joys. Happiness that at one time seemed but a faint dream can come true. The alternatives are no good and success is the only answer, success founded upon the principles given to us by God.

> Now may the God Who gives the power of patient endurance (steadfastness) and Who

supplies encouragement, grant you to live in such mutual harmony and such full sympathy with one another, in accord with Jesus Christ (Romans 15:5 AV).

May your marriage grow stronger each year; may you apply each new thing you have learned as you find the need; and may others, because of your love for Christ, ask you why you have the faith that you do.

MARRIAGE

From the Beginning
God created man and woman and blessed them, and called them Man from the start (Genesis 5:2 LB). (The word Man means both man and woman.)

God Made Woman
"This is it!" Adam exclaimed. "She is part of my own bone and flesh! Her name is woman because she was taken out of a man" (Genesis 2:23 LB).

God's Plan
But remember that in God's plan men and women need each other. For although the first woman came out of man, all men have been born from women ever since, and both men and women come from God their Creator (1 Corinthians 11:11 LB).

Loyalty
If you love someone you will be loyal to him no matter what the cost. You will always believe in him, always expect the best of him, and always stand your ground in defending him (1 Corinthians 13:7 LB).

Love
Love forgets mistakes; nagging about them parts the best of friends (Proverbs 17:9 LB).

Undemanding - Humble
Your attitude should be the kind that was shown us by Jesus Christ, who, though he was God, did not demand

and cling to his rights as God, but laid aside his mighty power and glory, taking the disguise of a slave and becoming like men (Philippians 2:5-7 LB).

Kindness
Kind words are like honey - enjoyable and healthful (Proverbs 16:24 LB).

Wisdom
A wise woman builds her house, while a foolish woman tears hers down by her own efforts (Proverbs 14:1 LB).

Full Life
The thief's purpose is to steal, kill and destroy. My purpose is to give life in all its fullness (John 10:10 LB).

READ Proverbs 31:10-31 in class.

War And Peace

Chapter 10

War and peace are at odds with each other. But as Christians trying to do God's will, we should realize that we will be tested. As Christians who understand God's goodness, and the peace of knowing about His power, we can feel as David did when he said:

> Lord, here in your Temple we meditate upon your kindness and your love. Your name is known throughout the earth, O God. You are praised everywhere for the salvation you have scattered throughout the world (Psalms 48:9,10 LB).

We can feel peaceful. But in real life situations, Satan says, "Kneel down and worship me!" These battle lines were drawn long ago between God and the serpent.

> Now the serpent was more subtle and crafty than any living creature of the field which the Lord God had made. And he (Satan) said to the woman, Can it really be that God has said, you shall not eat of every tree in the garden? (Genesis 3:1 AV).

And he says things to us today: "Can it really be that God has said, 'You shall not commit adultery?' Everyone else is doing it." Or, "Go ahead and take those supplies from your employer. He won't even miss them." Or as C. S. Lewis wrote in the SCREWTAPE LETTERS (speaking of New Christians): "As long as he retains externally the habits of a Christian he can still be made to think of himself as one who has adopted a few new friends and amusements but whose spiritual state is much the same as it was six weeks ago" (does not fully recognize sin and is not fully repentent). Or as Screwtape (Satan's name) says in another letter: "Catch the Christian at the moment when he is really being poor in spirit and smuggle into his mind the gratifying rejection, 'By jove/ I'm being humble!' "

So just as Eve didn't realize that she was directly opposing God when she made her choice, neither do we realize how those choices put us into the battle - ON SATAN'S SIDE. A serious and dangerous war is being fought every day of our lives and we are in it, on one side or the other.

> For we are not fighting against people made of flesh and blood, but against persons without bodies - the evil rulers of the unseen world, those might satanic beings and great evil princes of darkness who rule this world; and against huge numbers of wicked spirits in the spirit world (Ephesians 6:12 LB).

And as subtle and sneaky as this battle is at times, it is important that we realize how often we fight on Satan's side by opposing God.

My grandfather seemed to realize this battle was always being fought in our daily lives. I can remember him attributing many things to the devil. He would say in a sermon, "The devil is talking to you when you don't do what God has said to do." Or he would say to one of his children or grandchildren, "The devil's working on you." But many of us see this more like Flip Wilson when he says, "The devil made me do it." And we laugh it off, treat it as a joke, when in reality it is extremely important.

An article in the religious section of our daily paper had a few things to say about this importance: "Five million Americans plan their entire lives by the stars, according to Morris Cerulle, president of World Evangelism in San Diego. It's an effort of people for whom the God of the Bible has lost its authority. They are now searching for authority in the stars. Some say the occult - that fuzzily defined domain of the supernatural that includes witchcraft, astrology and satanism - threatens traditional religion. . .A couple of years ago, we in church viewed it as a passing fad. But obviously it's still with us and it's bigger than ever. THE OCCULT IS DIA-METRICALLY OPPOSED TO CHRISTIANITY. Devil worship can never replace worship of one God, a minister said" (Globe Democrat, Aug. 1972, "The Occult").

Of course you an I are immediately thinking that that doesn't include us. We are not worshipping Satan. But let's take a good look at the devil and how he works before we decide whether he takes over a part of our lives or not.

> The DARKNESS and GLOOM of Satan's king-doms (Colossians 1:13a LB). For you are the children of your father the devil and you love to do the evil things he does. He was a murderer from the beginning and a hater of truth - there is not an iota of truth in him. When he lies, it is perfectly normal; for he is the father of liars (John 8:44 LB).

Suppose you were the devil, fighting against God; would you only fight a little bit, or would you fight with all of your strength? Would you lie? In the serpent's first recorded battle he lied to Eve. Do you think he will tell the truth and play fair the rest of the time? He was not only a liar, he was sneaky. He told Eve to give the fruit to Adam. Why didn't he give the suggestions to Adam himself? Perhaps because he knew he had to sneak in through Eve or he couldn't win? Don't you know that the devil will continue to be sneaky?

I believe the forces of good and evil fight many battles; some of them small and sneaky, others are large and easy to see. But if I were the devil, I believe the best way to work up to the big battles, would be to begin small. I would tear out little pieces, not too close together, like in a square of paper. You probably remember doing this in school. In order to make a design we would cut little holes out in the fold of the paper and when it is opened up the holes are all over the square. But imagine that a person is involved and the devil is starting small, making little tears in our person. He rips little holes, not too close together, then he makes slashes, next he cuts out a circle; yet the person is still all in one piece, just as the piece of paper is all in one piece as long as the little holes, slashes and circles are unconnected. Perhaps in some places there is only 1/8th of an inch between the holes. The person might not even realize what is happening until suddenly the slightest pressure causes the paper to crumble and collapse. Then the person has also crumbled and collapsed. And that is when we see what looks to be the large battle. We see someone renounce God or commit murder or totally live their lives toward self-gratification. We can see that God has lost that battle but we have not seen all of the sneaky attacks that led up to the devil's victory. Any time I watch a sports game I think of the battle between God and Satan. Each team must work on the weaknesses of the other. The strongest team wins.

Of course, as Christians we understand that God is stronger than Satan. We know that because when Jesus came against Satan one day; when he was tested and tried on the mountain top, he won. We know that God is strongest because when Jesus was arrested, tried, crucified, and buried, he arose again from the dead. And Luke 22:53 tells us that Satan's power was supreme at that time. Yet he lost.

The only weakness God has is the weakness in us. The Scriptures point this out very thoroughly.

> For you are the children of your father the devil and you love to do the evil things he does. He was a murderer from the beginning and a hater of truth (John 8:44a LB).

> (But) he who commits sin (who practices evil doing) is of the devil - takes his character from the evil one; for the devil has sinned (**has violated the divine law**) from the beginning. The reason the Son of God was made manifest (visible) was to undo (destroy, loosen and dissolve) the works the devil [has done] (1 John 3:8 AV).

> But Peter said, Ananias, Satan has filled your heart. When you claimed this was the full price, you were **lying to the Holy Spirit**" (Acts 5:3 LB).

So we need to make the choice in the battle. One of the choices is to let Satan fill our heart causing us to lie to the Holy

Spirit. The other is to fight him constantly. Now apparently Ananias was a member of the church, but because he **allowed** Satan to fill his heart and because he lied to the Holy Spirit, he was killed. This is quite an example to us today, telling us to be careful that the same thing doesn't happen to us today. Satan works through men's hearts in small, subtle ways, asking us to forget about the truth, asking us to ignore what God has said, and asking us to lie to the Holy Spirit by telling ourselves that just one time won't matter, or by rationalizing our actions in some other way. When we rationalize even one small thing, we are allowing Satan to punch holes in our person and then because we have done wrong, we are even more vulnerable to let him make larger slashes in us.

> "In Montana, 23 year old Dean Baker, who claims to be a black magician and devil worshipper, murdered a social worker, cut his body into six parts, and as part of his own version of Satanic ritual, ate the heart" (Globe Democrat, Aug. 1972, "The Occult").

Of course you and I wouldn't do anything like that - not even near that horrible, terrible deed. But we need to honestly realize that the young man did not turn into a murderer suddenly. He began by letting Satan cut little holes in the paper. Perhaps he was made of very thin stuff to begin with; maybe his parents gave him no strength - no God to depend on. And the holes began, hate set in, the tears occurred, revenge and anger were added to hate; and finally total destruction happened to a young man only 23 years old. You and I were once on that same path of doom.

> Once you were under God's curse, doomed forever for your sins. You went along with the crowd and were just like all the others, full of sin, obeying Satan, the mighty prince of the power of the air, who is at work right now in the hearts of those who are against the Lord. All of us used to be just as they are, our lives expressing the evil within us, doing every wicked thing that our passions or our evil thoughts might lead us into. We started out bad, being born with evil natures, and were

under God's anger just like everyone else
(Ephesians 2:1-3 LB).

So how do we keep ourselves from being drawn back into
this horrible kingdom?

> So now we can tell who is a child of God and
> who belongs to Satan. Whoever is living a life
> of sin and doesn't love his brother shows that
> he is not in God's family; for the message to us
> from the beginning has been that we should
> love one another (1 John 3:10 LB).

The first commandment is that we love the Lord our God
with all our hearts, and the second one is that we love our
neighbor as ourself. We will be tested and tried in many ways
by Satan who will hope to make us quit loving our brother and
QUIT LOVING GOD. But we will win!

We know how happy they are now because they stayed true
to him. (James 5:11).

> [You should] be exceedingly glad on this
> account, though how for a little while you may
> be distressed by trials and suffer temptations,
> So that [the genuiness] of your faith may be
> tested, [your faith] which is infinitely more
> precious than the perishable gold which is
> tested and purified by fire (1 Peter 1:6,7a AV).

We will win because we are going to look to God!

> "They attacked when I was weakest but the
> Lord held me steady..." (Psalms 18:18 LB).

Trust in God will make us winners. But that trust covers
more than just blind following of principles that were handed
to us from our parents, from our church, from our friends, or
from our feelings. Trust in God means that we will trust in his
Holy Word and in it only. Whenever anything is presented to
us, we will check to see if what we see is what God wills to be
done.

One of the easiest ways to be tricked is to trust our own

feelings. Now don't misunderstand me; feelings and emotion are certainly a part of being a Christian. The New Testament tells about the early Christians being happy for one another, crying for each other, singing and making melody in their hearts. The devil's attack comes when he tries to make us believe that our feelings should be our guiding light. The "Jesus Movement" among young people is already being used by Satan to keep these young people away from God's truth. They originally turned to Jesus because He made them feel good. (He makes you feel great!) But then they turned completely toward their emotions as a guide, rather than turning toward God's Word as their principle rule. As one article put it, "We are touching the flip side of the Jesus movement."

They then become the turned-on generation, doing whatever turns them on. They want to hate - they hate. They want to fight - they fight. But the Bible doesn't tell us to do whatever we feel like doing. The devil tells us to do it; then he pays off in counterfeit money. I'll never forget the story of Nadab and Abihu, in the 10th chapter of Leviticus.

> But Nadab. and Abihu, the sons of Aaron, placed unholy fire in their censers, laid incense on the fire, and offered the incense before the Lord - **contrary to what the Lord had just commanded them!** So fire blazed forth from the presence of the Lord and destroyed them (Leviticus 10:1,2 LB).

Nadab and Abihu apparently decided that the Lord would be pleased with what they felt was pleasing. He wasn't. And we will remove a large weakness from within Satan's grasp if we never decide to do just what feels good to us, rather than checking to see if that is what God wants us to do. God's will versus our will - that's where the real battle always lies.

So if our lives are directed toward following God's will at all costs, we will be able to stand firm in the battle that is raging constantly within our hearts and our lives. We will be able to love our neighbor even when he isn't loveable, even when he doesn't believe the way we think is right, even when it is hard to love him. We will be a lot of things. We will be protected. As C. S. Lewis said in the Screwtape letters:

"Some humans are permanently surrounded
by it and therefore inaccessible to us."

Or as the scriptures explain it to us:

Last of all I want to remind you that your
strength must come from the Lord's mighty
power within you (Ephesians 6:10 LB).

So use every piece of God's armor to resist the
enemy whenever he attacks, and when it is all
over, you will still be standing up (Ephesians
6:13 LB).

You will need the strong belt of truth and the
breast plate of God's approval. Wear shoes
that are able (be prepared) to speed you on as
you preach the Good News of peace with God.
In every battle you will need faith as your
shield to stop the fiery arrows aimed at you by
Satan. And you will need the helmet of salvation and the sword of the Spirit - which is
the Word of God. Pray all the time. Ask God
for anything in line with the Holy Spirit's
wishes. Plead with him, reminding him of
your needs (Ephesians 6:14-18 LB).

Again, here is a list of the armor of God:

1. Truth
2. God's approval
3. Be prepared to preach the Good News
4. Faith
5. Salvation
6. The Word of God
7. Pray all the time

Decide right now that you will check your armor for any
missing pieces. When even one piece of that armor is missing
you are vulnerable and Satan has ground to work on.

TRUTH

Jesus Christ is the Way, the Truth, and the Life. Any man who comes to God must come through Jesus Christ. When you decided that you wanted a life after death - with God, did you proclaim your belief in Jesus Chist as the Son of God?

GOD'S APPROVAL

Looking for God's approval, we will remember that we are to love one another as God has loved us. And we will know without a doubt that we are not being loving when we have no time to be the woman that God wants us to be, when we are too busy to take care of our family as God has told us to, when we have no time to talk to our children, to listen to a neighbor, to help our husband. Satan likes to keep us running so that we will FEEL somewhat satisfied thinking we are really accomplishing something. But if we are not looking for God's will in our life, we are accomplishing nothing.

TELL THE GOOD NEWS

Our lives tell the Good News. Not only the marvelous news that we can be saved at death, but the tremendous news that we are being continually saved right now - by using God's help in our lives. And each person has a story they can tell others about. You can tell about how you found God's help in your life and what God means to you. Satan likes for us to think that we have to have all the knowledge in the world before we can begin to share the good news. And he is a liar.

FAITH

One day I was thinking about faith and I realized that I didn't know what faith really is. I remember praying that night, "God, help me understand what faith is. Give me this faith that some people seem to have." And right there I was taking a small step in faith. You can do that also. Then little by little you can learn to turn your whole life over to God. He is the great Shepherd and He knows how to take care of us.

SALVATION

One evening a friend called saying she really had a problem

and could I come over. She had been troubled for a few years, she said, about the fact that when she was baptized she had felt no guilt and had not recognized the fact that Jesus was saving her from sins she didn't feel she had. But she knew at the time that the Christian's life was good. It is an honest life and has association with people who are trying to be good. So she had entered into Christianity with the object of trying to live a good Christian life. She is a hard worker - loving, always ready to help others, always telling others about God. She seemed to be all of the good things we think of when we see a Christian woman. But she told me that just recently she began to realize that when people sang about Jesus, when they talked about "my Jesus", when they seemed to have a personal relationship with Him, she felt very left out.

This was because she didn't know Jesus as her Savior. And lately she had become more and more aware of the deficiencies in her life and began to feel the guilt she had never before experienced. SHE BEGAN TO SEE THAT WE ARE ALL SO UNLIKE GOD. She realized that she needed Jesus, desperately. So eight years after entering the church and accepting the "Christian life" she really found salvation.

She began a new relationship with Him. This time it was a relationship based upon solid ground - the Bible. This time it was based not upon her feelings but upon what God said to do.

So claim Jesus and salvation as the Bible describes it.

> "...'Brothers, what should we do?" And Peter replied, "Each one of you must turn from sin, return to God, and be baptized in the name of Jesus Christ for the forgiveness of your sins; then you shall also receive this gift, the Holy Spirit. For Christ promised him to each one of you who has been called by the Lord our God, and to your children and even to those in distant lands" (Acts 2:37b-39 LB).

WORD OF GOD

God talks to us about many things through the Holy Scriptures. We learn how he wants us to live and we learn what will make us happy. The scriptures thoroughly furnish us to every good work, so as we study them we will grow in the knowledge of what God is like and what He wants us to do. Satan likes for us to read the Bible by skipping over all of the things that we don't want to do. But because the Bible reveals God to us it also reveals how tremendously he loves us. And we can look at the things that seem hard to do, knowing that they are there for our benefit, because He loves us so much.

PRAYER

Here with that wonderful conversation with God we can wrap up everything else in a blanket of peace. We can ask God for wisdom and understanding. We can ask him to help us with our weaknesses and temptations. All of our problems can be handled by God. He is most wondrously able. Praise His Holy name!

Is it possible to be daily involved in a war - and still have PEACE? Many of us have found the peace that passeth understanding. How can we describe it? Words fail. You will have to experience it yourself. You will need to look at life as God's garden. And when God plants a garden - flowers bloom.

GOD'S PLAN

To each minute part of life
God has a plan in mind.
The sunshine down on earth below
To brighten our bleak days,

It brings us needed warmth at times
And cheerful illuminous rays.
With the sun he sent the rain
To dampen new mown hay,

A drink to give a thirsty plant
And puddles in which to play
Days and Nights are in this plan,
The nights to give us peaceful rest.

Each day we labor til we tire
And look til even tide.
He sends us sorrow on our way
To strengthen our souls and yet,
He brings us happiness in part
To forget our broken hearts.

In each and every day we trod
We need to stop and think
That God has plans for each of us
And Order from the start.

Libby Palmer

Don't worry about anything; instead pray about everything; tell God your needs and don't forget to thank him for his answers. If you do this you will experience God's peace, which is far more wonderful than the human mind can understand. His peace will keep your thoughts and your hearts quiet and at rest as you trust in Christ Jesus (Philippians 4:6,7).

WAR AND PEACE

Satan Will Lose
How you are fallen from heaven, O Lucifer, son of the morning! How you are cut down to the ground - mighty though you were against the nations of the world. For you said to yourself, "I will ascend to heaven and rule the angels. I will take the highest throne" (Isaiah 14:12,13 LB).

He Is Crafty
The serpent was the craftiest of all the creatures the Lord God had made (Genesis 3:1 LB).

We Can Fight on His Side
For you are the children of your father the devil and you love to do the evil things he does. He was a murderer from the beginning and a hater of truth - there is not an iota of truth in him (John 8:44 LB).

When He Fills Our Hearts
But Peter said, "Ananias, Satan has filled your heart.

When you claimed this was the full price, you were lying
to the Holy Spirit" (Acts 5:3 LB).

Temptation Not From God
And remember, when someone wants to do wrong it is
never God who is tempting him, for God never wants to
do wrong and never tempts anyone else to do it (James
1:13 LB).

We Can Win
I advise you to obey only the Holy Spirit's instructions.
He will tell you where to go and what to do, and then you
won't always be doing the wrong things your evil nature
wants you to. For we naturally love to do evil things
that are just the opposite from the things that the Holy
Spirit tells us to do; and the good things we want to do
when the Spirit has his way with us are just the opposite
of our natural desires. These two forces within us are
constantly fighting each other to win control over us, and
our wishes are never free from their pressures (Galatians
5:16,17 LB).

Be Careful
Be careful - watch out for attacks from Satan, your great
enemy. He prowls around like a hungry, roaring lion,
looking for some victim to tear apart (1 Peter 5:8 LB).

Trust God's Love For Us
For I am convinced that nothing can ever separate us
from his love. Death can't and life can't. The angels
won't, and all the powers of hell itself cannot keep God's
love away (Romans 8:38 LB).

Trust God's Strength
Last of all I want to remind you that your strength must
come from the Lord's mighty power within you
(Ephesians 6:10 LB).

Have God's Peace
If you do this you will experience God's peace, which is
far more wonderful than the human mind can understand.
His peace will keep your thoughts and your hearts quiet
and at rest as you study in Christ Jesus (Philippians
4:7 LB).

SUGGESTED READING LIST

1. *The Christian's Secret of a Happy Life,* by Hannah Whithall Smith
2. *Person to Person,* by Bobbie Lee Holley; R. B. Sweet
3. Faith Alive Growth Group Series; R. B. Sweet
4. *Halley's Bible Handbook,* by Henry Halley; Zondervan
5. *What's So Great About the Bible,* by James C. Hefley; David C. Cook Pub. Co., Elgin, Illinois
6. *A Life With Wings,* by Marge Green; Quality Printing Co., Abilene
7. *The Power of Positive Thinking,* by Norman Vincent Peale; Prentice Hall, Inc.
8. *The Art of Understanding Yourself,* by Cecil Osborne; Zondervan
9. *Prayer: Conversing With God,* by Rosalind Rinker; Zondervan
10. *Prayer, the Mightiest Force in the World,* by Frank C. Laubach; Fleming H. Revell Co.
11. *Beyond Ourselves,* by Catherine Marshall; Fleming H. Revell
12. *Fascinating Womanhood,* by Mrs. Helen B. Andelin; Pacific Press
13. *The Art of Understanding Your Mate,* by Cecil Osborne; Zondervan
14. *Guide to the Christian Faith,* by William A. Spurrier; Charles Scribner's Sons
15. *Living Happily Ever After,* by Bob Mumford
16. *God Owns My Business,* by Stanley Tam/Ken Anderson; Word Pub.
17. "The Screwtape Letters," in *The Best of C. S. Lewis,* by C. S. Lewis; Christianity Today, Inc.